XML
A Guide for Librarians

Ron Gilmour

Guide #11

a division of the AmericanLibraryAssociation
Chicago and London

ISBN 0-8389-8255-7

Printed in the United States of America

05 04 03 02 01 5 4 3 2 1

table of contents

introduction

This material is the result of a number of LITA Regional Institutes that I taught during 2002 and 2003. This publication is a neatened and somewhat polished version of my lecture notes and betrays its origin in at least two ways. First, the style is a bit more casual than is traditional for technical writing; I hope that this will convey something of the spontaneity of the workshop environment. Second, because these lectures were delivered in the context of a one-day program, I have not attempted to teach you everything about XML. Let me reiterate: this work is in no way intended to be comprehensive. This reflects the amount of material that I felt a motivated workshop participant could digest in the course of a day. What I hope to accomplish in the current work is to give you a gentle introduction to XML and some related technologies and provide you with some tools that will allow you to continue your studies. There are many good books and Web resources available that will provide more complete coverage. Here, I hope to teach you the basics of an important technology and help you to understand its unique relevance to librarianship and other information professions.

All of the example files from this book are available online at http://web.utk.edu/~rgilmou1/xmlbook.

Ron Gilmour

chapter 1

XML and the Nature of Markup

As much as I would like for us to begin with fresh, open minds, this is simply not possible, because what we are discussing is perhaps the most intensely hyped technology to come along since the Web itself (or at least since Java). This hype has been pervasive and very effective. I often meet people who clearly have very little idea of what XML actually is, but they are nevertheless convinced that they should be using it for whatever project they are currently involved in.

What I hope to accomplish in this guide is to teach you something about what XML is, what it can do, and what is involved in using XML in the real world . . . specifically, the real library world. I hope that this will give you enough understanding of XML to cut through some of the hype and critically evaluate whether XML is a tool that may be useful in your work. My goal is not to sell you on XML. If this guide allows you to make the informed decision that XML really isn't the thing for your current projects, that's fine. Hopefully you will keep XML in mind and it will be in your toolkit for when you are presented with new projects. At the very least, you should be better able to understand the people in your systems departments, vendor representatives, and other IT professions who you come in contact with when *they* talk about XML.

The first thing that I would like to tell you about XML is that it is really simple. XML is a simple language based on the principle of calling a spade a spade—I think that this is a quality that librarians especially will appreciate. XML should clarify, not obscure.

The fundamental purpose of good markup is to clarify meaning and facilitate intelligent use of information. I think that XML is therefore very much in line with the values that libraries stand for. That's one reason I think that XML is the legitimate business of librarians—this is what we're already good at!

Second, I'd like to warn you that **XML is a way of structuring data**, a means of recording or storing information. It does not, by itself, *do* anything in particular. (But don't worry, there are loads of technologies built up around XML that *do* all sorts of things.) When we hear about new technologies (especially Web technologies), our (understandable) tendency is to ask what they do. Can it animate my images? Will it make my Web page look glitzy so my boss will be impressed? Will it entice wealthy alumni to donate to my library? XML by itself does none of the above; in fact it doesn't really *do* anything. Why not?

History and Relationships of Markup Languages

XML doesn't do anything because it is a markup language. Within computer technology we can divide the "languages" that we hear so much about into two types: programming languages, which describe procedures; and markup languages, which describe data.

Markup languages allow us to add a layer of what we might call metadata (or perhaps commentary) on top of the text or data that we are working with. For instance, it could allow us to distinguish one type of text from another (e.g., a red letter Bible distinguishes between words spoken by Christ and those spoken by anyone else). In going through textbooks we might highlight the important points in yellow, so we are literally "marking up" or labeling text as either very important or (by default) less important.

The computer markup technologies that we will be discussing today are all based on something called SGML (Standard Generalized Markup Language), a system in which the metadata is enclosed in little things with angled brackets called "tags." So, if we want to say that a particular word is important, we might enclose it between two of these "tags," like this:


```
<important>word</important>
```

Markup vs. Meta-Markup

Most of us are familiar with the idea of using a markup language. When we mark up a document in HTML, we do not have to think about what goes between the angled brackets. The tags are created for us. An external power (namely the W3C or World Wide Web Consortium) has decreed that an HTML document should use some or all of a set of about 100 tags in a certain way. Our work as authors is simply to apply those tags intelligently to the document at hand. HTML is an example of a markup language.

Standard Generalized Markup Language (SGML), on the other hand, is a metalanguage. It does not define particular tags (elements). It allows us to define our own tags, making us producers of the language, not just consumers.

So, in figure 1, SGML appears as an area, a region of potential markup languages, and HTML as a discreet point, an already defined markup language. HTML can be thought of as an instance of SGML. Other instances include the Text Encoding Initiative (TEI), Encoded Archival Description (EAD), and many other languages.

SGML, frankly, is hard. It offers a huge number of options that can be used to customize a markup language for a specific purpose. Due to its complexity, which translates to a large

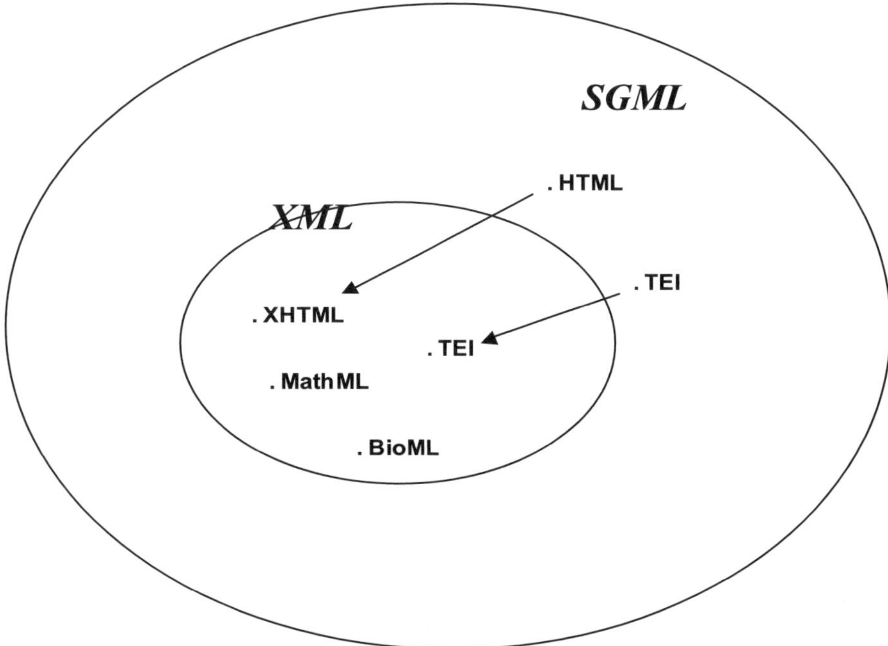

figure 1: In this diagram, metalanguages (SGML and XML) are shown as areas, while actual markup languages based on those metalanguages are shown as points within the area.

start-up investment, it only really caught on in a few industries. It only came to the attention of the general public when HTML was developed. HTML had the virtue of being simple, but this also resulted in HTML documents being comparatively information-poor.

XML is a streamlined subset of SGML. Many of the little-used and complex features of SGML have been removed, leaving a lightweight but still very flexible metalanguage. XML is much easier to use than SGML, both from the viewpoint of the document author and from that of the software developer who has to write software to do things with documents, and XML was designed specifically with the Web in mind.

In figure 1, XML is shown as an area rather than a point to indicate that it is still a metalanguage. It is shown entirely enclosed within SGML because it is a proper subset of SGML. Therefore, a valid XML document is automatically also a valid SGML document (but not the other way around!).

So, the big secret is that the hot new technology called XML has: (a) not undergone substantial change since 1997; and (b) wasn't really new then, since it is just a stripped-down version of a technology that dates back to 1969.

Semantic vs. Presentational Markup

I said earlier that HTML documents are generally information-poor. What did I mean by that? Why is it true? In order to answer this question, we must discuss two general styles of markup: semantic and presentational. In presentational markup, we use tags for the merely cosmetic purpose of defining how the content is going to look, for example:

<paragraph>My object in coming here was to see the great beds of shells, which are elevated some yards above the level of the sea. They nearly all consist of one species of <italic>Erycina</italic>; and these shells at the present day live together in great numbers, on the sandy flats.</paragraph>

or

<block align="left">
3 Winding Brook Dr.<lineBreak />Guilderland, NY 12084
</block>

In semantic markup, we use tags to add meaning to the document, for instance:

<paragraph>My object in coming here was to see the great beds of shells, which are elevated some yards above the level of the sea. They nearly all consist of one species of <taxonomicName rank="genus">Erycina</taxonomicName>; and these shells at the present day live together in great numbers, on the sandy flats.</paragraph>

or

<address>
<street>3 Winding Brook Dr.</street>
<city>Guilderland</city>
<state>NY</state>
<zip>27516</zip>
</address>

Sometimes you will hear people describe HTML as a presentational markup language and XML as semantic. It is best to think of markup languages as existing somewhere along a continuum between the purely presentational and the purely semantic. HTML is about 80% presentational: most of the tags provide instructions for how something should be visually rendered by a Web browser. But some provide hints at meaning. H1 causes the text to be displayed in large, bold type, but also provides the semantic information that this is a top-level descriptor for a section of a document. Note that in the above examples from Darwin's *Voyage of the Beagle,* "paragraph" tags occur both in the semantic and in the presentational examples, because a paragraph is a construct with both semantic and presentational aspects. (A paragraph is a semantic structure, but the rules regarding how a paragraph should look are so well established that people now confound the appearance with the fact. Most HTML authors have used <p> tags where no real paragraph was present.) XML has the *potential* to be 100% semantic, but in practice most XML-compliant languages will have some presentation-oriented features, for example TEI's "render" attribute. Some XML-based languages are even *primarily* presentational, for example XSL-Formatting Objects.

It is possible to write HTML that is fairly semantically rich, mostly by using the universal "class" attribute combined with the presentationally generic "span" and "div" tags, but very few people do this. The span tag describes a line of "inline" text (i.e., no line break afterward), while "div" describes a textual "division," separated from like divisions by a line break.

Here is an example of a Chinese restaurant menu as it might appear marked up for simple display on the Web:

```
<html>
<head>
<title>Chinese Menu</title>
<!–This example shows normal, semantically poor HTML. –>
</head>
<body>
<b>Subgum Wonton</b>- Crabmeat, sliced chicken, roast pork, shrimp, lobster,
imported straw mushrooms, bamboo shoots, waterchestnuts and Chinese veg. baby
corn, served with crispy wonton. <b>$9.15</b>
<br>
<b>Chicken with Orange Flavor</b>- Tender fillets of marinated chicken, delicately
sauteed and seasoned w. imported orange peels. <b>$8.30</b>
<br>
<b>Seafood Wor Bar</b>- Crabmeat, squid, shrimp, scallops, lobster with mixed vegeta-
bles served with sizzling rice. <b>$10.10</b>
<br>
<b>Sauteed Steak Kew in Hunan Style</b>- Choice beef steak sauteed with various veg-
etables in spicy sauce. <b>$9.15</b>
<br>
<b>Dragon and Phoenix</b>- General Tso's Chicken and Hot and Spicy Shrimp.
<b>$8.90</b>
</body>
</html>
```

The name of each item and its price are in bold and there's a break before we go on to the next item. An item would appear in the browser as:

Dragon and Phoenix- General Tso's Chicken and Hot and Spicy Shrimp. **$8.90**

Here is the same menu, still in HTML, but enhanced with some semantic markup:

```
<html>
<head>
<title>Chinese Menu</title>
<!–This example shows how HTML can be made semantically rich through use of the
universal class attribute. –>
</head>
<body>
<div><span class="item_name">Subgum Wonton</span>- Crabmeat, sliced chicken,
roast portk, shrimp, lobster, imported straw mushrooms, bamboo shoots, waterchest-
nuts and Chinese veg. baby corn, served with crispy wonton.
<span class="price">$9.15</span></div>
<div><span class="item_name">Chicken with Orange Flavor</span>- Tender fillets of
marinated chicken, delicately sauteed and seasoned w. imported orange peels.
<span class="price">$8.30</span></div>
```

```
<div><span class="item_name">Seafood Wor Bar</span>- Crabmeat, squid, shrimp,
scallops, lobster with mixed vegetables served with sizzling rice. <span
class="price">$10.10</span></div>
<div><span class="item_name">Sauteed Steak Kew in Hunan Style</span>- Choice beef
steak sauteed with various vegetables in spicy sauce. <span
class="price">$9.15</span></div>
<div><span class="item_name">Dragon and Phoenix</span>- General Tso's Chicken and
Hot and Spicy Shrimp. <span class="price">$8.90</span></div>
</body>
</html>
```

Here, the "class" attribute is used to say what kind of information is contained in the "span" tags. "Span" is used purely as a container tag and has no presentational effect.

Finally, here is the menu as a purely semantic XML document–the tags only indicate what the various pieces of information are, not how they should look:

```
<?xml version="1.0"?>
<menu>
<!–This is fully semantic XML –>
<menu_item>
<item_name>Subgum Wonton</item_name>
<item_description>Crabmeat, sliced chicken, roast portk, shrimp, lobster, imported straw
mushrooms, bamboo shoots, waterchestnuts and Chinese veg. baby corn, served with
crispy wonton. </item_description>
<price>$9.15</price>
</menu_item>
<menu_item>
<item_name>Chicken with Orange Flavor</item_name>
<item_description>Tender fillets of marinated chicken, delicately sauteed and seasoned
w. imported orange peels. </item_description>
<price>$8.30</price>
</menu_item>
<menu_item>
<item_name>Seafood Wor Bar</item_name>
<item_description>Crabmeat, squid, shrimp, scallops, lobster with mixed vegetables
served with sizzling rice. </item_description>
<price>$10.10</price>
</menu_item>
<menu_item>
<item_name>Sauteed Steak Kew in Hunan Style</item_name>
<item_description>Choice beef steak sauteed with various vegetables in spicy
sauce.</item_description>
<price>$9.15</price>
</menu_item>
<menu_item>
<item_name>Dragon and Phoenix</item_name>
<item_description>General Tso's Chicken and Hot and Spicy Shrimp. </item_description>
<price>$8.90</price>
</menu_item>
</menu>
```

Generally speaking, we can think of documents with semantic markup as being "smarter" or more information-rich than those with presentational markup. Presentational markup is geared to a single type of use: italicized text has little meaning if the document is being read by a voice browser, but if we mark the text as "french" or "emphasized" this might provided some clues that any application would be able to work with.

This is what is meant when people talk about the separation of style and content. Stylistic information is often application-specific, while the content may have more general utility, so separating them creates greater flexibility. (This argument will sound familiar if you've ever learned about Cascading Style Sheets for use with HTML.)

Frankly, doing good semantic markup is a bit harder than doing presentational markup. When Web authors mark up a document in HTML, they check to make sure it looks okay in the major browsers and, if so, then it's good enough. They don't usually stop to ponder questions about how the document might be interpreted by other types of applications or whether our markup would be meaningful to a person who finds this document thirty years from now.

This is another goal of XML: creating coded documents that are readable both by people and machines. This sounds like hype, and it has certainly been used that way, but think about the amount of time you have spent in your life trying to convert a file from one format to another. Since XML is fairly readable even as "raw" code, it should never become unusable, even without appropriate software.

A related hypish phrase you will hear about XML is that it produces "future-proof" documents. Most of us have some old documents that we can no longer make use of because absolutely no one has retained a copy of the clunky old software that created the file. If the software had created the file in XML, we wouldn't have a problem because anything that can read ASCII can read the file, so such a file would be somewhat usable as long as the ASCII standards hold.

(Aside: XML is actually based on a character encoding standard called Unicode, which should ideally include all characters in known languages, including Klingon. Since Unicode is a superset of ASCII, a Unicode-compliant editor will still be able to read and write ASCII documents, so for the purposes of this book, we will pretend that XML is just ASCII.)

chapter 2

XML Syntax and Well-Formedness

Now that, hopefully, you understand the desirability of using some type of semantic markup, let's take a look at how to actually create XML documents.

No special software is needed to create XML documents. You can use a simple text editor, even something as basic as Notepad. If you find yourself hand-coding XML with any frequency, you'll probably want to find something a little fancier. Textpad and Notetab are two of the more robust Windows text editors that are sometimes used for XML.

An XML document consists of the following parts:

1. an XML declaration
2. a document type declaration
3. elements
4. attributes (these are really parts of elements)
5. entity references
6. comments
7. processing instructions

Six out of the seven are optional—you can have a perfectly good XML document that consists of nothing but elements, as in the Chinese menu example above.

XML Declaration

The first item, the XML declaration, is an optional item whose main function is simply to identify this as an XML document. In its simplest form, it looks like:

```
<?xml?>
```

Generally, this is expanded somewhat to include the version of XML used, and sometimes the type of character encoding used. These are specified using name/value pairs called "pseudo-attributes." A third optional pseudo-attribute is "standalone," which indicates whether or not the present document is dependent upon any external files. So, a long XML declaration might look like.

```
<?xml version="1.0" encoding="UTF-8" standalone="yes"?>
```

Document Type Declaration (or Doctype)

The document type declaration indicates what type of document this is and where information about documents of this type may be found. It usually takes the form:

```
<!DOCTYPE menu SYSTEM "menu.dtd">
```

Here, "menu" tells you that this is a "menu" document, and that therefore the root element of this document must be "menu." "SYSTEM" tells you that the file should be looked for externally, and "menu.dtd" is the name of the file containing information on the tags used in the document.

Note that you should not refer to the Document Type Declaration by the obvious acronym, because DTD is used to refer to the Document Type *Definition*, which is the file referred to by the Document Type Declaration.

Sometimes, the document type declaration actually contains the structural information itself rather than pointing to another file that contains it, but this seems to mostly be used in textbook examples.

Elements

Elements are the real "meat" of an XML document. An element consists of an opening tag, a closing tag, and whatever content comes between the two. The content may consist of text (character data), or of more elements, or both. Elements are the only truly required part of an XML document: you can have a perfectly good (meaning well-formed) XML document that contains nothing but elements.

Note that while you will sometimes hear people use the terms "element" and "tag" interchangably, this is not really correct, as an element consists of a pair of tags, plus the content between them.

Attributes

Attributes take the form of name/value pairs, like the "pseudo-attributes" in the xml declaration. (Those are called "pseudo-attributes" because a true attribute must by definition be associated with an element.) You'll be familiar with these from HTML as things like:

```
href="http://www.google.com"
```

or

```
src="picture.jpg"
```

Attributes do not stand alone, but must be "attached" to an element, appearing within the element's opening tag. An element may have multiple attributes, as in the common HTML construct:

<img src="apple.jpg" height="210" width="430" alt="picture of an apple">

Attributes are often used to qualify or add information to an element, often the sort of information that you might not want displayed. This is due to the fact that web browsers generally don't display attributes.

Entity References

Entity references are a way of reading content from external files into the document, similar to Server Side Includes which are used with HTML. They take the form:

&something;

that is, an ampersand sign followed by a string of characters, usually a mnemonic name for the thing being included, and ending with a semi-colon.

Entity references are used in HTML for escaping markup related characters, such as "<" for the less-than sign, and for specifying special characters, such as "é" for a letter e with an acute accent, but in XML their role is much greater. Rather than a single character, an entity reference could specify a whole file, so you could have:

©rightStatement;

or

&hamlet;

A common use is for bits of boiler-plate text that appear in many different locations, especially if they undergo frequent change. We'll discuss these in more detail when we talk about writing Document Type Definitions.

One use of entity references is to glue smaller documents together to make a "virtual" large document. This is one of the reasons that the XML declaration is optional, allowing numerous XML documents to be pulled together using entity references without creating multiple XML declarations in the resulting document.

Comments

Happily, comments in XML work exactly as they do in HTML:

<!–my comment –>

Processing Instructions

Processing instructions, or PIs, are instructions that should be passed to a particular type of software. You can think of them as comments meant for XML processing software rather than for people. The only use of PIs that I will discuss here is linking an XML document to a stylesheet. This takes the form:

```
<?xml-stylesheet type="text/css" href="stylesheet.css"?>
```

Note that syntactically this looks just like the XML declaration. Nevertheless, the authors of XML insist that the XML declaration is an entirely different thing and is *not* a type of PI.

This is a small document that uses all of the parts we have discussed:

```
<?xml version="1.0" encoding="UTF-8"?>
<!DOCTYPE note SYSTEM "note.dtd">
<?xml-stylesheet type="text/css" href="notestyle.css"?>
<note type="informal">
<!—This is a comment. —>
This is a short XML document with all the basic parts &amp; pieces.
</note>
```

By way of review, the first line is the XML declaration, with pseudo-attributes indicating the version and the encoding scheme used. The second line is the DOCTYPE declaration, which states that the present document follows the structure defined in the file "note.dtd." The third line is a processing instruction telling whatever software reads this document that it should display the document in accordance with the rules contained in the file "notestyle.css." The fourth line contains the opening tag of a "note" element, which has an attribute called "type" with the value of "informal." Then we have a comment, some content (which contains an entity reference that will produce an ampersand in the output), and a closing tag for the note element.

Well-Formedness vs. Validity

XML defines two levels of "correctness" for a document. In order to qualify as an XML document at all, the document must be *well-formed.* This means that the document's syntax conforms to the XML 1.0 standard published by the W3C. When I was first learning about XML, it was not clear to me why we needed a term (and an awkward term at that) simply to indicate that an XML document follows the XML standard. The reason is that "well-formedness" is actually a revolutionary concept that is one of the few truly new things in XML.

In SGML, there is no such thing as a well-formed document. In order to be a "good" SGML document, the document must conform to some Document Type Definition (DTD), not just to the syntactic rules of SGML. Conformance to a Document Type Definition is known as validity. In SGML, a document is either valid or invalid. The concept of well-formedness gives XML authors the option of "winging it"—marking up a document in a way that makes sense without going to the considerable trouble required to find, write, or modify a DTD.

With reference to figure 1, you can think of a well-formed document as occupying space within the XML circle, but not corresponding to any particular dot within that circle, so a sort of "generic" XML document.

To be well-formed, a few rules must be followed. These are the ones that are specific to XML and that may not be familiar to HTML authors.

1. **All elements must have closing tags (except in the case of empty elements, where the terminal slash is used to indicate opening and closing within a single tag).**
   Examples: <speciesName>Magnolia grandiflora</speciesName>
   <horizontalRule />
   <horizontalRule/>
   The space prior to the terminal slash is optional. Many XML authors have gotten in the habit of using it because it allows you to write valid XHTML which will display correctly in non-XML aware browsers such as Netscape.
2. **All attribute values must be quoted (using either single or double quotation marks).**
   Example: <img src="apple.jpg" />
3. **All elements must be strictly nested.**
   Right: <a><b>content</b></a>
   Wrong: <a><b>content</a></b>
   Another way to think of this: no element may contain a fraction of another element. This makes XML documents describable through a parent/child or tree/branch/leaf metaphor.
4. **Each document must have a single element that encloses the entire content of the document (like the <html> element in HTML).**
   This element is called the root element. For some reason this rule is frequently forgotten by beginners.
5. **Element names are case sensitive.**
   You are free to use whatever case conventions you like in naming elements, but an element "P" is different from "p," so <P>text</p> is wrong.

A criticism that is sometimes leveled against XML is that it is terribly strict and nitpicky about syntax. This is true (although I don't see that it is markedly more true for XML than for a number of other languages), but this pickiness is for a reason. It may make life a little harder for document authors, but it makes things much easier for programmers who are writing software to do things with XML. Why should we care about making life easier for programmers?

Once upon a time, there was an SGML application called Encoded Archival Description (EAD), which will be described in more detail later on. A number of archives started making EAD documents available on their Web sites, directing users to download a free SGML viewer called Panorama. Panorama was then bought by a company who no longer wanted to give it away for free, leaving the archives in an embarrassing bind. One of the original goals of the authors of XML was that a good programmer should be able to write an XML parser within a couple weeks. So, as long as an undergrad can write a parser in a couple weeks, no one can have a monopoly on XML! Strict syntax translates to highly predictable documents, which translates to ease of writing parsers, so the "strictness" that people sometimes complain about is one of the very things that ensures that XML is free and open. Note that software that deals with full-blown SGML tends to be pricy (because SGML parsers are hard to write), while lots of XML software is free.

A Simple XML Application

Let's say that we have a bunch of information and we would like to make different subsets of that information available separately. For instance, let's say that we have a list of all the books that your library has cataloged in the past week and we want to send out friendly "new book" lists to faculty members in various departments. We might start out with a list of all the new books. Such a list might look something like this (with apologies for the simplistic bibliographic records):

```
<?xml version="1.0" encoding="UTF-8"?>
<newbooks>
<!--full file available as nbwf.html -->
<book subject="biology">
<title>The art of seeing things : essays</title>
<author><firstname>John</firstname> <lastname>Burroughs</lastname></author>
<imprint>Syracuse, N.Y. : Syracuse University Press, 2001</imprint>
<callnumber>QH 81 B914 2001</callnumber>
</book>
<book subject="biology">
<title>Ecosystem dynamics of the boreal forest : the Kluane project</title>
<author><firstname>Charles J.</firstname> <lastname>Krebs</lastname></author>
<imprint>Oxford ; New York : Oxford University Press, 2001</imprint>
<callnumber>QH 106.2 Y84 E36 2001</callnumber>
</book>
<book subject="chemistry">
<title>The weak hydrogen bond : in structural chemistry and biology</title>
<author><firstname>Gautam R.</firstname> <lastname>Desiraju</lastname></author>
<imprint>Oxford ; New York : Oxford University Press, c1999</imprint>
<callnumber>QD 461 D44 1999</callnumber>
</book>
<!--more books here -->
<book subject="biology">
<title>Encouraging diversity : the conservation and development of plant genetic
resources</title>
<author><firstname>Conny</firstname> <lastname>Almekinders</lastname></author>
<imprint>London : Intermediate Technology, 2000</imprint>
<callnumber>QK 981 A46X 2000</callnumber>
</book>
<book subject="math">
<title>Microstructural characterization of materials</title>
<author><firstname>David</firstname> <lastname>Brandon</lastname></author>
<imprint>Chichester, [England] ; New York : J. Wiley, 2001, c1999</imprint>
<callnumber>TA 417.23 B73 2001</callnumber>
```

</book>
</newbooks>

This document has a very simple structure. There is, of course, a single root element called "newbooks" that encloses everything else. This root element contains child "book" elements. Each "book" element contains child elements of types "title," "author" (which in turn contains first name and last name), "imprint," and "call number." In addition to its child elements, the "book" element also has a "subject" attribute, with values such as "biology" and "chemistry."

Note that, as in HTML, the spacing and line breaks are purely for my own sanity. The document will be processed just the same even if the whole thing were typed on one line.

Currently, Microsoft Internet Explorer (IE) is the most XML-aware browser available. Using IE6 is a good quick way to see if your XML document is well-formed. If I change the document so that it is no longer well-formed, you'll see that IE6 will then give me an error message and won't display the document.

Here, I have removed the closing "title" tag from the first book, resulting in the error message in figure 2.

For viewing in a browser, XML must be used in combination with style sheets. Remember that with HTML, we work with a fixed set of tags that will be understood by any HTML browser. We cannot reasonably expect that the developers of IE6 could

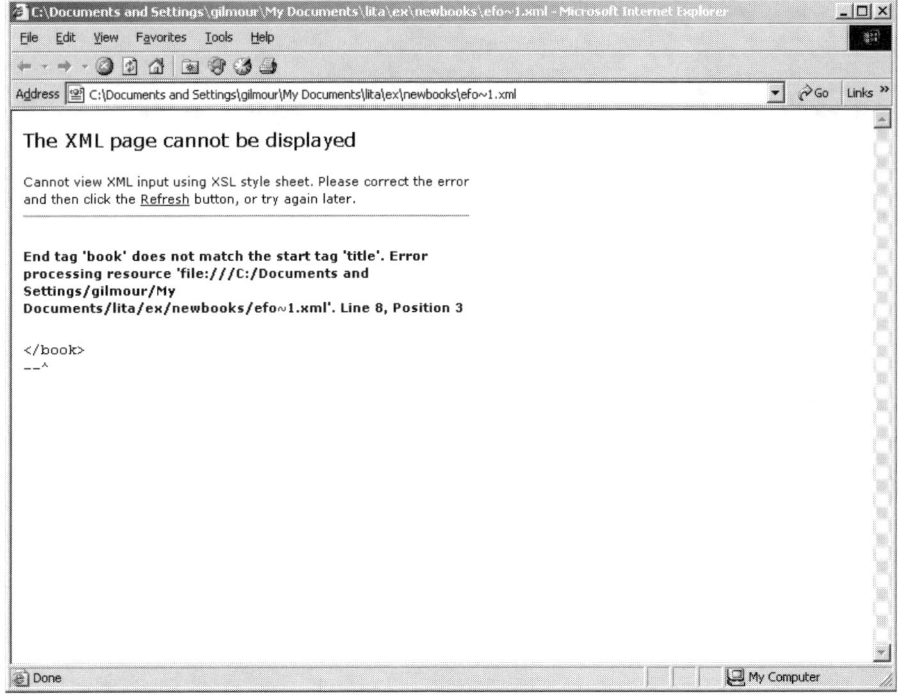

figure 2: Internet Explorer will not display an XML document unless it is well-formed.

know that we would create the present XML document using tags like "newbooks." So, IE6 has a default method of displaying a document in which all elements are displayed the same way. To make IE6 to do anything different with an element, we must provide instructions in the form of a style sheet. Style sheets are covered in some detail in Chapter 4. For now, just know that stylesheets can be used to affect how an XML document looks in a browser.

By using a very simple stylesheet with the present document, we can make it appear in IE6 as shown in figure 3.

"Okay," you say, "but I could make something that looks like that using plain HTML." The added value of XML is that it gives us the power to use the content of this document as a data source. By applying another style sheet, we can make the very same document render as shown in figure 4, sorting the books by the last name of the author.

More to the original purpose, we can make it display such that only the books with a subject attribute value of "biology" are displayed (this is still sorting by author's last name, see figure 5).

We can also do a fair amount of tweaking with respect to the display options—figure 6 shows an example where just the chemistry books are displayed, but in a tabular format.

Remember that all of these screen shots are just various renditions of the single plain text file that we typed at the beginning.

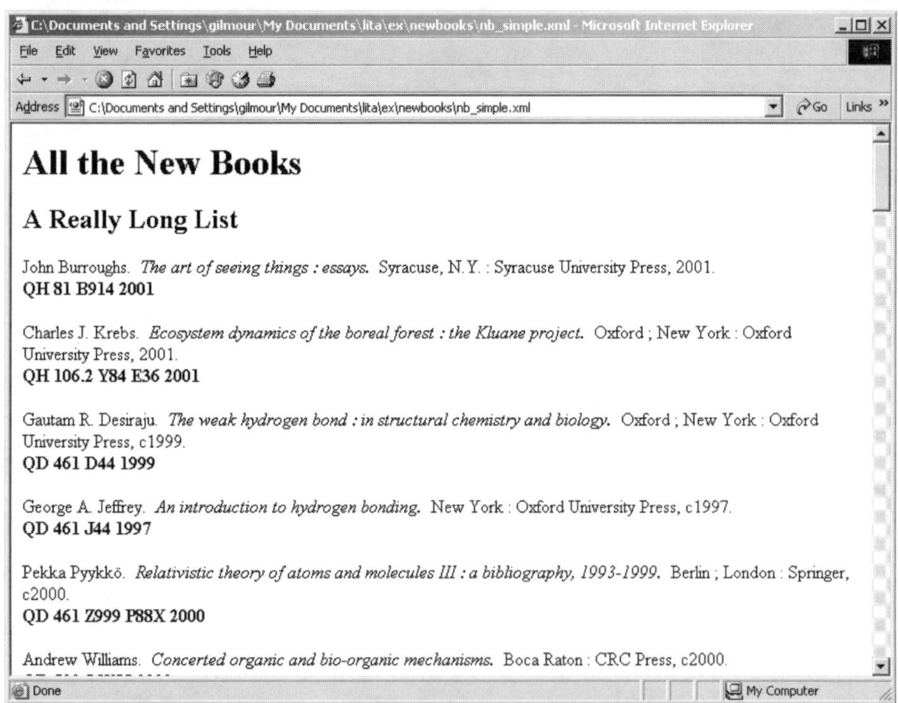

figure 3: New books list displayed with a simple CSS stylesheet.

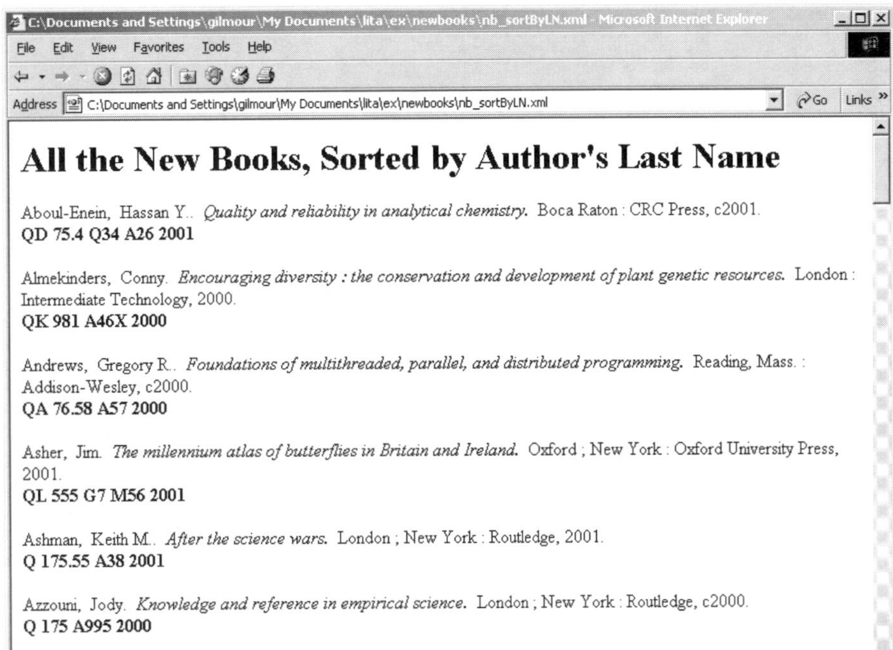

figure 4: New books list displayed using an XSL stylesheet to sort by author's last name.

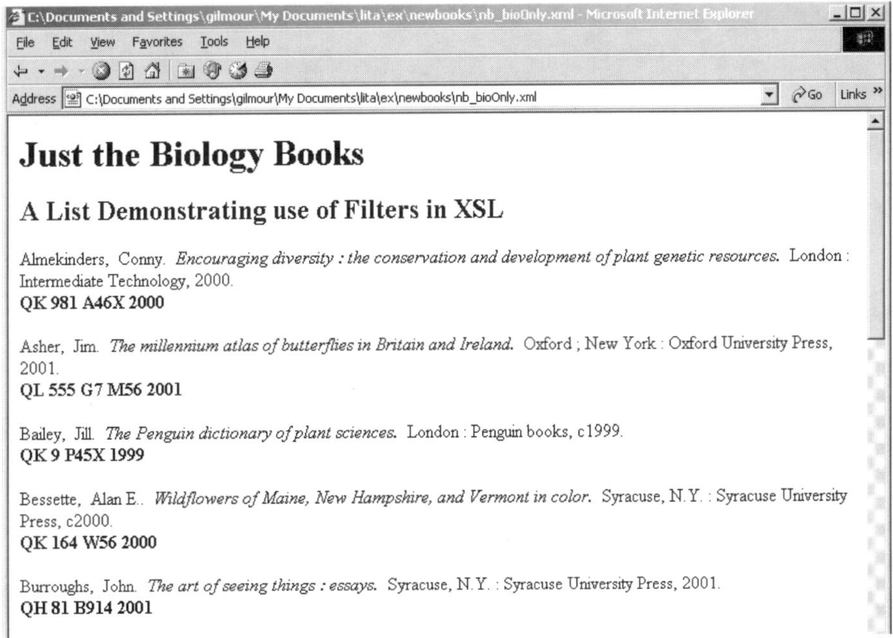

figure 5: New books list displayed using an XSL stylesheet to show only the biology books.

Just the Chemistry Books

This time, the list as an HTML table, with many attractive fea through the magic of Cascading Style Sheets

Aboul-Enein, Hassan Y.	*Quality and reliability in analytical chemistry*	Boca Raton : CRC Press, c2001
Desiraju, Gautam R.	*The weak hydrogen bond : in structural chemistry and biology*	Oxford ; New York : Oxford Universit Press, c1999
Eustathopoulos, Nicolas	*Wettability at high temperatures*	Amsterdam, [The Netherlands] : New York ; Oxford : Pergamon, c1999
Jeffrey, George A.	*An introduction to hydrogen bonding*	New York : Oxford University Press, c1997
Pyykkö, Pekka	*Relativistic theory of atoms and molecules III : a bibliography, 1993-1999*	Berlin ; London : Springer, c2000

figure 6: New books list displayed using an XSL stylesheet to show only the chemistry books, with additional formatting.

chapter 3

Enabling Data Sharing

Validity, Entities, and DTDs

Recall the two levels of "rightness" in XML. The first, and minimal, level is well-formedness. To even legitimately call a document an XML document, that document must be well-formed (i.e., conform to the XML 1.0 spec).

The second level of "rightness" is validity. Validity refers to following rules specific to a certain flavor of XML. For instance, in order to have a "good" TEI document, that document must not only be well-formed; it must also conform to the rules and structures laid out by TEI. You can think of XML that is merely well-formed as being "generic" XML and valid XML as being more specific.

The rules that a document should follow in order to be a valid instance of a particular XML-based markup language are referred to as a *schema*. In HTML, to take a familiar example, an LI element (list member) should only be used inside of either a UL or OL element, not outside of one. That rule is specified in the schema for HTML.

The most common way of documenting these kinds of rules is something called a Document Type Definition (or DTD). DTDs can be either very simple or very complex. Very general applications such as TEI often have immense DTDs with hundreds of declarations, but we are mostly going to look at short, simple DTDs.

So let's say that you have mastered the construction of well-formed XML documents following all the rules in the XML 1.0 spec. Now I'm telling you that you can write documents that follow even more rules! Why should you be excited about this?

At the simplest level, this takes us back to the idea of document predictability. If you are writing a program that manipulates XML documents in some way it can be useful to be able to assume something about the structure of the document. If the document is valid XHTML, for instance, you only need to code for the possibility of encountering LI elements once you are inside an OL or UL element, not while you are inside a P element. By validating first, you avoid having to write error-catching code that says what the program should do when it encounters an LI element inside an P element.

The larger scale reason why validity is interesting is that it enables data sharing. If you come up with a brilliant method of encoding résumés in XML, that's great, but with DTDs you can document your work and you can share these rules with other interested parties; for instance, job applicants. You could allow prospective applicants the option of downloading your résumé DTD and then they can send you their résumé in the form specified by the DTD. Perhaps most importantly, they have available to them any number of free software products and Web services that will allow them to validate their work against your DTD so they can see if they've got it right. Now that you, as the employer, have all of your résumés submitted so that they conform to a single DTD, you can easily write software to do things with those résumés. You could write stylesheets that would display the candidate names in decreasing orders of years of experience, etc. In short, you would have an applicants database without anyone having to key all the data from the résumés into a database. Some publishers are experimenting with systems like this, where they provide an article DTD and authors are expected to submit their work such that it validates against that DTD. In cases like this there would probably be editing software involved so that the writer would not necessarily have to actually read the DTD, but could just write and the editor would take care of the markup details.

Element Declarations

For a simple example, let's say that we want to write a DTD for an HTML unordered list (just a UL element containing some number of LI elements and nothing else).


```
<UL>
<LI>milk</LI>
<LI>bread</LI>
</UL>
```

DTDs consist of declarations of elements, attributes, and entities. For the list example, we'll only be dealing with elements (which are the easiest to declare). We need to declare both elements. Generally, the order of your declarations doesn't matter—I tend to take a top-down approach, so I'll start with UL. The basic formula that we use to write an element declaration is:

```
<!ELEMENT elementName elementContentModel>
```

The "content model" part means that we say something about what the element will contain.

So, our element declaration for the UL element would look like:

```
<!ELEMENT UL (LI+)>
```

This indicates that our document may contain elements named UL and that these UL elements must contain one or more LI elements.

We would then declare our "li" element by saying

```
<!ELEMENT LI (#PCDATA)>
```

The content of an LI element is just plain text, and the way we say that in DTD language is #PCDATA ("parsed character data").

So we now have a very simple example of a DTD and a document that follows its rules.

There are two ways in which we can indicate that this DTD is to apply to this document. The first (and generally best) we have already seen: we can use a DOCTYPE declaration to tell the XML processor that the document should be validated against our DTD. In this case, our simple list document would look like this:

```
<?xml version="1.0"?>
<!DOCTYPE UL SYSTEM "list.dtd">
<UL>
<LI>milk</LI>
<LI>bread</LI>
</UL>
```

Note that this assumes that the two declarations above are saved in a file called "list.dtd" and that this file is in the same directory as the present document. The other possibility would be to include the DTD within the document itself.

```
<?xml version="1.0"?>
<!DOCTYPE UL [
<!ELEMENT UL (LI+)>
<!ELEMENT LI (#PCDATA)>
]>
<UL>
<LI>milk</LI>
<LI>bread</LI>
</UL>
```

This isn't done very often in the "real world": after all, the main point of a DTD is that it can be shared among numerous documents. Including the DTD in the document itself is handy while you are developing a DTD, to minimize flipping back and forth between two files trying to get them to agree.

There are a few basic types of element content models with which you should be familiar. One of the most common types is a sequence of child elements, for example:

```
<!ELEMENT address (street, city, state, zip)>
```

This means that the address element must contain the four child elements listed, in the order that they're listed, and none of them may occur more than once. That last item is an important point: when you list a child element without indicating otherwise, you are saying "exactly one occurrence." You can indicate other possibilities using a plus sign to indicate "one or more" (required and repeatable; as we did in the "list" example), an asterisk to indicate "zero or more" (optional and repeatable), or a question mark to indicate "zero or one" (optional and not repeatable) (see figure 7).

Another common construction is a list of alternatives that may be used, in which case the vertical line or pipe character replaces the comma. For example:

```
<!ELEMENT spouse (husband | wife)>
```

This means that the spouse element may contain exactly one husband element OR exactly one wife element.

Sequences and lists of alternatives are often used in combination, for instance:

```
<!ELEMENT person (name, address, job*, (husband | wife)?, child*)>
```

This says that a person element must contain a single name, a single address, may contain zero or more jobs, may contain either a husband or a wife, and may contain any number of children.

A couple other types of element declarations that you should be aware of are the unrestricted element (designated by the keyword ANY), and the empty element (designated by the keyword EMPTY). Note that when you use the ANY designation, it means that the element may contain any *declared* child element, it does not give you free reign to make up elements. With reference to empty elements, remember that these may still have attributes. "Empty" only indicates a lack of content, and attributes are not considered content.

```
<!ELEMENT vague ANY>
<!ELEMENT void EMPTY>
```

Finally, a very common construction is mixed content, especially when dealing with documents that fall into the realm of "text" more than data. "Mixed content" refers to a situation where an element contains both text (PCDATA) and other elements. To take another HTML-esque example, let's say that we want to write a rule for a paragraph element that will allow the paragraph to contain bold or italic text if necessary. We could write this as:


```
<!ELEMENT paragraph (#PCDATA | italic | bold)*>
```

This syntax confuses people, but think of it this way: the paragraph element contains a possibly infinite sequence of children, each of which may be either text, an italic element, or a bold element.

Attribute Declarations

Attribute declarations are a little more involved than element declarations, and they also allow for some pretty neat tricks that are not possible using elements alone.

No indicator	Exactly one
+	One or more
*	Zero or more
?	Zero or one

figure 7: Numeric indicators for DTDs.

The generic form of an attribute declaration is as follows:

```
<!ATTLIST elementName attributeName type "default value">
```

Remember that attributes do not exist on their own but must be tied to particular elements, so elementName refers to the element to which the declared attribute will be tied. The attributeName is just that. The type allows you to specify a little bit about what is allowed in your attribute. There are a number of different attribute types and some of those are very rarely used, so only the most common ones will be described here.

The single most common attribute type is CDATA, which is yet another way to say "text." So, a simple case of declaring an ISBN attribute for a "review" element might look like this:

```
<!ATTLIST review isbn CDATA #REQUIRED>
```

Another very common attribute type that is similar to CDATA but a little more restrictive is NMTOKEN, which prevents spaces from being in the value (so that might actually be a better type for ISBN). Instead of declaring one of the pre-defined types, you can also insert a pipe-delimited list of values into the type slot, meaning that the attribute must take one of those values. So, for example:

```
<!ATTLIST review genre (fiction | nonfiction) "fiction">
```

This means that a "review" element has a genre attribute that may take either the value fiction or nonfiction. If the genre attribute is not present, it will default to "fiction."

```
<?xml version="1.0" encoding="UTF-8"?>
<!DOCTYPE reviews [
<!ELEMENT reviews (review+)>
<!ELEMENT review (#PCDATA)>
<!ATTLIST review genre (fiction | nonfiction) "fiction">
]>
<reviews>
<review genre="nonfiction">Highly informative, yet boring.</review>
<review>I laughed, I cried, it was better than Cats.</review>
</reviews>
```

Note that this document (see figure 8) specifies no attribute value for the second review, but in IE6 the attribute has been written in. (This tells us that IE6 contains what we call a "validating parser," meaning that it actually looks at the DTD.)

As implied by the term "ATTLIST," you can declare more than one attribute within a single declaration, and this is how they are usually done, a single ATTLIST declaration including all the attributes for a particular element.

```
<!ATTLIST journal issn NMTOKEN #REQUIRED
  coden NMTOKEN #IMPLIED>
```

This example also illustrates the REQUIRED and IMPLIED keywords, which may take the place of a default value. IMPLIED means "optional." So this declaration indicates that a "journal" element must include an "issn" attribute and may optionally have a "coden" attribute.

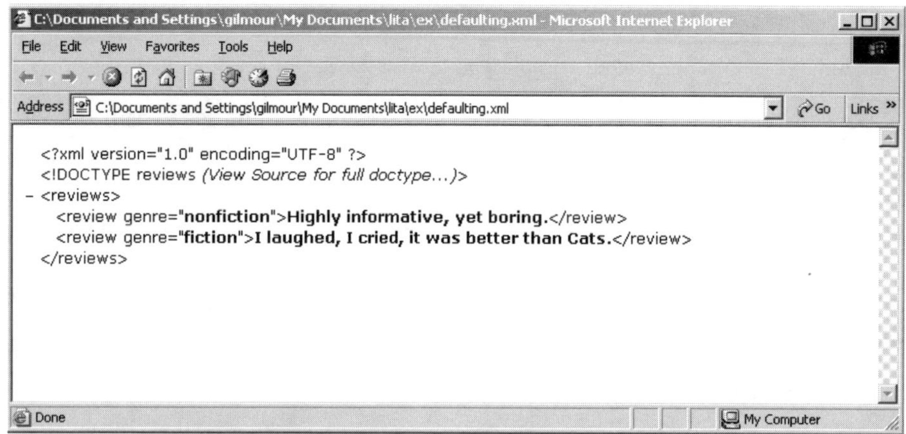

figure 8: Internet Explorer displaying a default value provided by the DTD

There are two more attribute types that I'd like to mention. There is a type called ID that means that the value of that attribute can not be duplicated for any two like elements in the document, so, in database terms, an attribute of type ID would serve as a unique identifier for whatever element it is attached to. (There is also an inexplicable rule associated with these that the value of an ID-type attribute may not begin with a number.)

There is a corresponding type called IDREF. The value of an attribute of type IDREF must be the value of some other element's ID-type attribute. So ID and IDREF attributes together provide a neat means for creating associations between elements and coding relational data in XML.

Johann Sebastian Bach is known for having written a truly huge amount of music during his lifetime, but he was no masochist. He frequently re-used music that he had written to set new texts. An extreme example of this is his Christmas Oratorio, in which a large portion of the music is drawn from three secular cantatas from earlier in his career.

In the Web page shown in figure 9, the individual movements of the early cantatas and the oratorio are linked to each other using ID and IDREF attributes. I've used a combination of XSL stylesheets and JavaScript to create an effect such that when you mouse over one column of the page, the corresponding movements are highlighted in yellow in the other column. The relevant part of the DTD looks like this:

```
<!ATTLIST movement id ID #REQUIRED
  model_movement IDREF #IMPLIED
  parody_movement IDREF #IMPLIED>
```

This states that each movement *must* have a unique attribute called "id" and that it *may* have either a "model_movement" (indicating a backward temporal relationship) or a "parody_movement" (indicating a forward relationship). The value of either the "model_movement" or the "parody_movement" attribute would have to be the value of the "id" attribute of another movement.

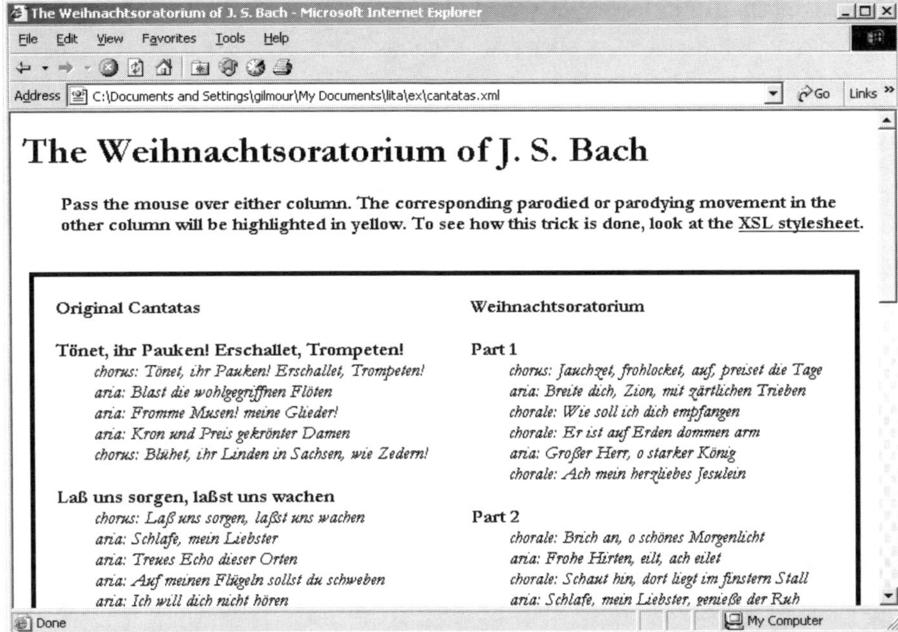

figure 9: ID and IDREF attributes can be used to create logical links between related elements.

Child Elements vs. Attributes

If you construct XML documents with any frequency, you will often find yourself wondering whether a particular bit of information should be coded as a child element or as an attribute. For instance, if you want to express the idea that a book has an ISBN, you could code that either as:

```
<book><isbn>087220538X</isbn></book>
```

or:

```
<book isbn="087220538X" />
```

Stated more generally, the idea that "A has a B of C" can be coded either using a child element:

```
<A><B>C</B></A>
```

or using an attribute:

```
<A B="C" />
```

There is rarely a definitive "right" answer to the question of how to code such information, but it is useful to be familiar with the differences between the two approaches so that you can make an informed decision.

Probably the most important of these differences is that attributes allow you to do some very primitive sorts of data-typing (saying what *kind* of content the attribute value should contain). For instance, you cannot define an element such that no spaces may be contained in the content, or such that the content must be one of a known list of values, or such that a default value is defined.

Another difference that is a bit trivial is that technically attributes do not have an order, so information where order is not important may be better stored in attributes. I have an addressbook file in XML that mostly codes data about my friends as elements. I often have to peek at the DTD to see whether "email" or "phoneNumber" comes first, when really it shouldn't matter.

Coding something as an attribute will usually save you a few characters (no end tag), which could add up in really large documents. Attributes do not allow for hierarchical content, so, for instance, if you decide to code a street address as an attribute, it would not be easy to go back later and break it up into city, state, zip, etc.

Finally, for a given element, attributes are not repeatable, so you can have a "correspondent" element with five different "email" child elements, but that element could only have one "email" attribute. Attributes have some special qualities that you can make use of in creative ways, so please remember this and put some thought into your decisions about whether to code something as an element or attribute. For more on the child element versus attribute quanadry, see Simon St. Laurent's *XML Elements of Style* (Neal-Schuman, 2002).

Entity Declarations

You now know how to declare your elements and attributes, so all that remains are entities, which are fairly simple. The basic formula is:

```
<!ENTITY entityName "whatever will replace the entity reference">
```

If you want to simply use an entity reference to replace a bit of text, you declare that as:

```
<!ENTITY spe "M. E. Grenander Department of Special Collections and Archives">
```

If this declaration is included in the DTD, then we can simply type "&spe;" when we want to say "M. E. Grenander Department of Special Collections and Archives."

Viewed in IE6, this short document

```
<?xml version="1.0" encoding="UTF-8"?>
<!DOCTYPE sample [
<!ELEMENT sample (#PCDATA)>
<!ENTITY spe "M. E. Grenander Department of Special Collections and Archives">
]>
<sample>
The German intellectual emigre collection is housed in the &spe;.
</sample>
```

appears as shown in figure 10.

To read the content of an external file into the document, declare the entity as follows:

```
<!ENTITY warAndPeace SYSTEM "warAndPeace.txt">
```

This provides the basis for a handy trick that can be used to associate a single XML document with multiple stylesheets. If you declare the content of your document as an entity, you can then create multiple "minidocuments" that refer to it (see figure 11).

If, for instance, your carefully XML-encoded data is in a file called "rarebooks.ent," (I use the ".ent" extention to indicate xml files that may not be well-formed on their own, but will be when used appropriately via an entity reference) you could then associate that file with a stylesheet in a document like this:

```
<?xml version="1.0" encoding="UTF-8"?>
<!DOCTYPE rarebooks SYSTEM "rarebooks.dtd">
<?xml-stylesheet type="text/xsl" href="rb1.css"?>
<rarebooks>&rarebooks;</rarebooks>
```

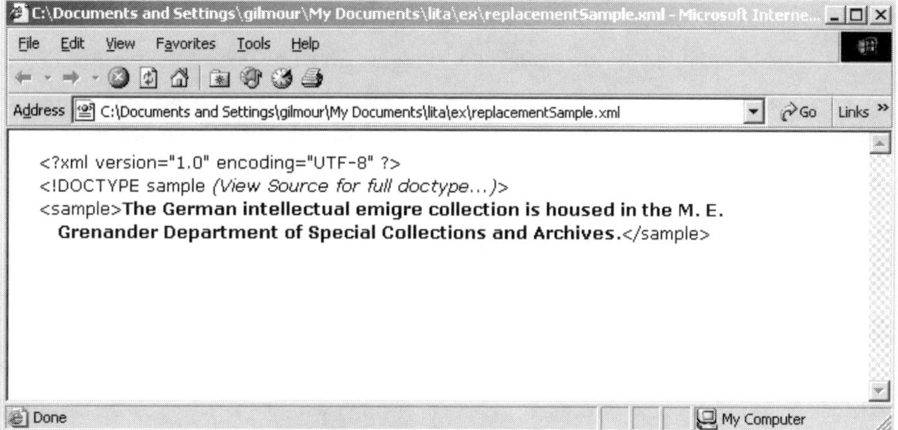

figure 10: Using an entity reference for text substitution.

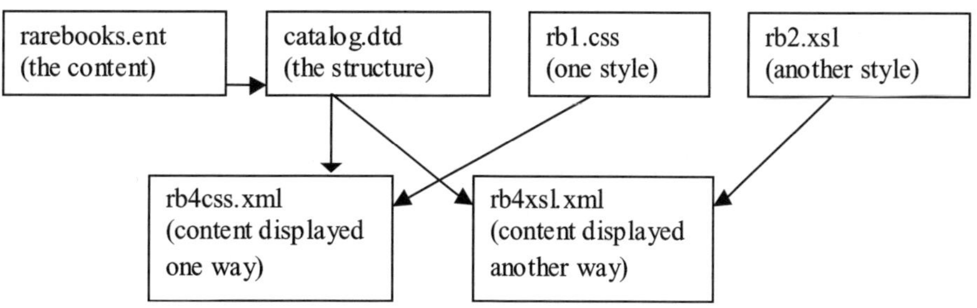

figure 11: Using an entity reference to couple an XML-encoded content document with various stylesheets.

The entity reference to the file would be included within “rarebooks.dtd.” You could create any number of these little files to associate the same data with any stylesheet.

A word of caution here: entities in XML are very powerful and can do a great deal to make your data more modular, but do remember the issue of human readability. If your documents are mostly little bits of code pointing to other documents, that's not very readable, so think about this before you develop really complicated content-management systems based around entities.

We already mentioned the use of entities for dealing with special characters in HTML. You can do this in XML as well, but it isn't “built in,” so you have to declare the special characters yourself, *except* in the case of five special entities that are built into the standard: <, >, “, ‘, and &. Any of these may be called with the same entity reference as is used in HTML without having to declare it:

```
&     &amp;
<     &lt;
>     &gt;
'     &apos;
"     &quot;
```

For special characters, you have two choices. You can just use the ASCII (or Unicode) decimal value for the character in your content, or you can declare mnemonic forms in your DTD so you can remember them. You would do the latter like this:

```
<!ENTITY eacute "&#233;">
```

This would then allow you to use é to produce a small “e” with an acute accent.

Parameter Entities

The entities we have talked about so far are called general entities and are often used to facilitate the reuse of XML content. There is another class of entities, called parameter entities, that perform the same function for DTDs themselves, allowing you to reuse groups of declarations.

The formula for declaring a parameter entity is:

```
<!ENTITY % entityName "replacement text">
```

Parameter entities are called using a percent sign rather than an ampersand. Often they are called immediately after they are declared.

Let's say that you really like being able to use the mnemonic names for special character entities in XML documents. You want to be able to do this regardless of what DTD you are using. You could put all of your special character entity declarations in a file called, say, “specialCharacters.ent.” Then, if you want to make those declarations accessible for a document using your “bibliography.dtd,” you would add the following lines to bibliography.dtd:

```
<!ENTITY % specialCharacters "specialCharacters.ent">
%specialCharacters;
```

Another possibility that you can imagine is that if you make use of various types of documents, many of which might contain addresses, you could write a separate, short address DTD and then use that in all the other documents. This would also ensure that addresses were encoded the same way on "invoice" documents as on "memo" documents.

Validation on the Desktop

IE6 automatically checks XML documents for well-formedness and will not display badly formed files. With the addition of a tiny plug-in, it may also be used to check the validity of XML documents. The URL for downloading the plug-in is www.microsoft.com/downloads/details.aspx?FamilyId=D23C1D2C-1571-4D61-BDA8-ADF9F6849DF9&displaylang=en. (The Microsoft Web site changes frequently, so if this URL doesn't work, go to www.microsoft.com and type "Internet Explorer Tools for Validating XML and Viewing XSLT Output" into the search box.) This tool will add a "validate XML" option to the "right-click" menu in IE.

Going back to the silly "reviews" example:

```
<?xml version="1.0" encoding="UTF-8"?>
<!DOCTYPE reviews [
<!ELEMENT reviews (review+)>
<!ELEMENT review (#PCDATA)>
<!ATTLIST review genre (fiction | nonfiction) "fiction">
]>
<reviews>
<review genre="nonfiction">Highly informative, yet boring.</review>
<review>I laughed, I cried, it was better than Cats.</review>
</reviews>
```

If I display the document in Internet Explorer and right-click anywhere on the document, I get a menu with "Validate XML" as one of the choices (see figure 12).

If I choose the "Validate XML" option, a window pops up that tells me "Validation Successful" (see figure 13).

To demonstrate, let's change the value of the first review's "genre" attribute from "nonfiction" (a legal value per the DTD) to "documentary," an illegal value (see figure 14).

Now the document will still display in IE (because it's still well formed), but if I check the validity, I get an error message telling me that "Attribute 'genre' has an invalid value according to the DTD/Schema." There are some XML validating services available on the web that will allow you to validate by uploading local files. The W3C has a validator at http://validator.w3.org and Brown University's Scholarly Technology Group offers one at www.stg.brown.edu/service/xmlvalid.

XML Applications

Now that we have learned a bit about what is involved in developing a "flavor" of XML for use with a particular type of document, let's take a look at some of the XML applications that are particularly relevant for the library world.

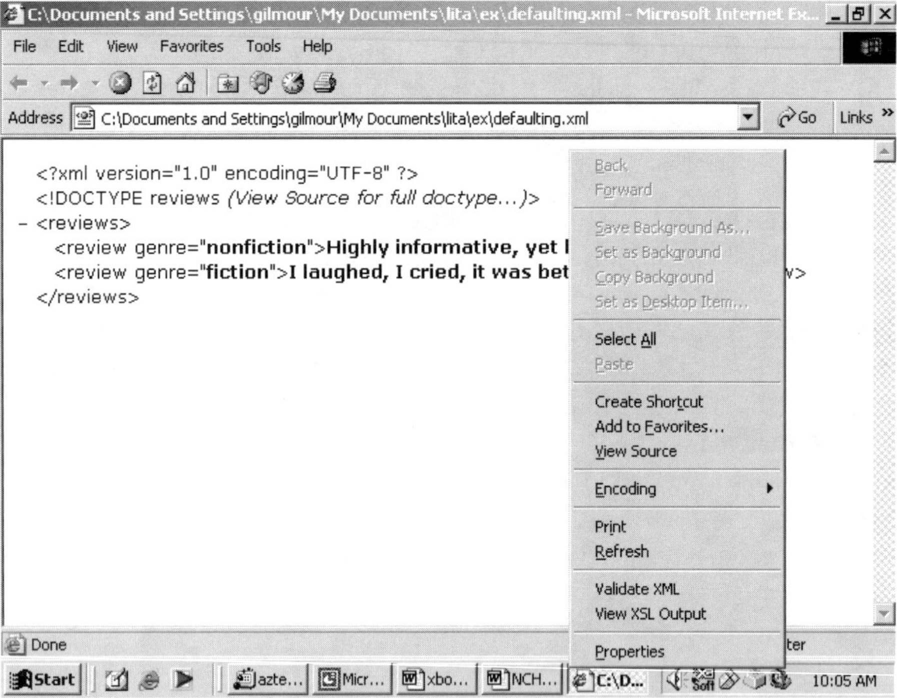

figure 12: Internet Explorer's right-click menu when the XML tools are installed.

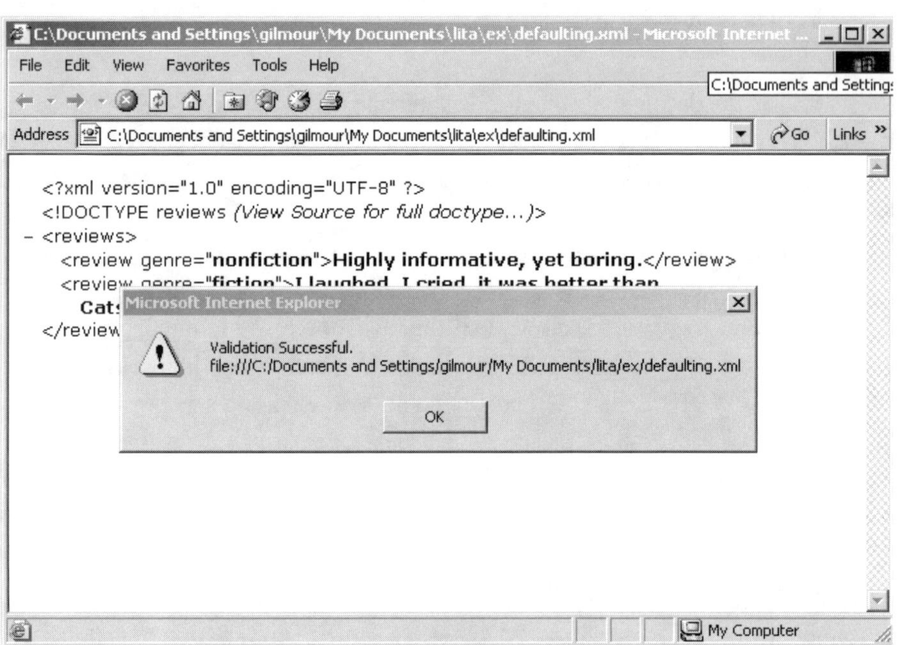

figure 13: Successful validation message in Internet Explorer.

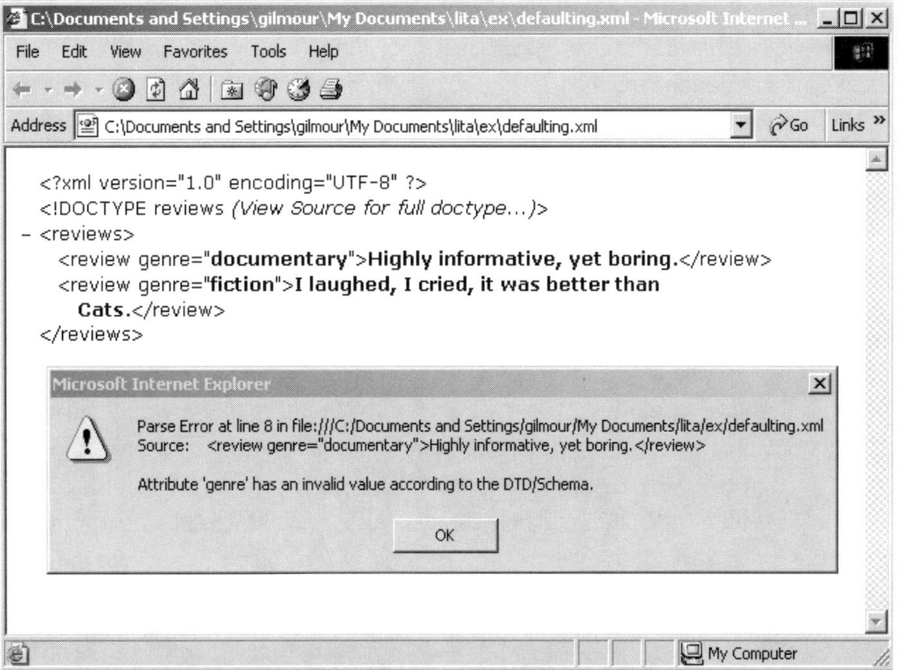

figure 14: Unsuccessful validation message in Internet Explorer.

Roy Tennant edited a very interesting book called *XML in Libraries* (Neal-Schuman, 2002) that includes first-hand accounts of various real-world XML library-related projects. In this book, he categorizes the projects under seven headings:

- Using XML in Library Catalog Records
- Using XML for Interlibrary Loan (arguably a special case of #7)
- Using XML for Cataloging and Indexing (metadata, searching)
- Using XML to Build Collections
- Using XML in Databases
- Using XML for Data Migration
- Using XML for Systems Interoperability

I'm not going to go through these in any systematic way, but I thought that this list might serve to arouse curiosity and creativity. Frankly, the vast flexibility of XML makes trying to enumerate its possible uses a bit like enumerating the possible uses of an alphabet, but for library applications, the section headings of Tennant's book offer a good starting point.

Using XML in Library Catalog Records: XML-MARC

MARC has been with us for quite a while now and will likely be with us (in some form) for quite a while longer. Some people, therefore, get a bit overexcited when we talk about anything happening to MARC. Unfortunately, at some point there was a lot of very enthusiastic talk about how XML would *replace* MARC. In my opinion, XML is no more likely to *replace* MARC than it is to *replace* HTML; it may, however, change how MARC looks (just as it has changed how HTML looks). What we have to remember here is that MARC is two things: a data model and a syntax (or way of expressing instances of that data model). So, XML-MARC is just a change in the syntax, not the data model. So we'll still have a 245 subfield a, it just might look like this

```
<datafield tag="250">
<subfield code="a">1st ed.</subfield>
</datafield>
```

instead of like the MARC records that we are familiar with.

The advantage of moving to an XML version of MARC is that it would move the library's data into a format that would be more in keeping with the rest of the world. XML has been called the *lingua franca* of data interchange, while MARC records as they exist now are used by libraries and only libraries. Also, since XML is hierarchical, it may provide a way to make hierarchical MARC records, which could be useful for the cataloging of Web sites.

The XML-MARC idea is still in its formative stages, and it will be really interesting to see how this develops in the coming years. The Library of Congress has also developed a standard called MODS (Metadata Object Description Schema; see www.loc.gov/standards/mods) that can be seen as a more generalized form of XML-MARC to cover media types that are not well served by traditional MARC fields. MODS uses "real word" element names rather than MARC's numeric tags. Even more general in scope is the METS project (Metadata Encoding and Transmission Standard; see www.loc.gov/standards/mets), which includes tags for administrative and structural metadata as well as descriptive.

I would also like to point out that not all the work on this is being done at the Library of Congress and in fact a lot of experimental work with XML-based MARC cataloging has happened at Stanford as part of the Lane Medical Library's Medlane project, so if you're interested in XML-MARC, you'll definitely want to look at the Web sites for both LOC and Stanford.

The Text Encoding Initiative

TEI is an interesting example of a very general purpose markup language. It is designed for use with anything that could be considered a "text." TEI is particularly designed to facilitate the scholarly analysis of texts, so it is a good candidate for a way to mark up something like the contents of a medieval manuscript with glosses, theological texts with layers of commentary, or a variorum edition that combines the features of a number of different editions. TEI also has the distinction of being possibly one of the most important computing initiatives to come out of the humanities.

TEI has an immense DTD, but this has been made highly modular, so that there is a fundamental part of the DTD (containing large-scale elements like "text" and "corpus") as well as a number of sections that apply only to certain types of texts, such as dramatic works, dictionaries, or poetry. These may be freely mixed, so you can come up with the minimal DTD that you need for your purposes (the full DTD is about 72K). TEI even has a Web-based system called the Pizza-Chef that allows you to generate this DTD online. (The name refers to the fact that you have the basic part of the DTD, or crust, combined with whatever "toppings" you want.)

In addition to what TEI allows scholars to do with the text itself, TEI includes a very robust metadata structure, the TEI Header. There are projects that actually use this format for metadata even if they don't actually do TEI markup. The TEI header allows editors/taggers to include a lot of information not only about the print source used for the encoded version, but also details of the encoding process (e.g., were spelling errors retained or corrected), tagging policies, amount and variety of coffee drunk by the encoder during the procedure, etc.

Many digital library projects are using TEI as the basis of their work. The TEI Web page currently lists 107 projects. Some of the better known include the *Perseus Digital Library* in ancient Greek literature (out of Tuft's University), the Library of Congress's *American Memory*, Brown University's *Women Writers Project*, and UNC Chapel Hill's *Documenting the American South*.

TEI actually predates XML. Like many XML applications, it began as an SGML application that has recently been reformulated into XML (but many of the projects are still mostly SGML-encoded). For quite a while, if you wanted to use XML with TEI, you had to actually use a subset called TEI-Lite, but now the entire TEI element set is available for XML, which is a great accomplishment.

TEI was designed to provide scholars with a set of tools for analyzing texts, so the way a document is marked up will often depend on the kinds of questions that the researcher wants to ask. There can be no single, definitive TEI markup for a given document. A person studying, for instance, inter-gender dialogue in Dickens would code the works quite differently from someone studying Dickens' use of mythological allusions.

Encoded Archival Description

TEI is a good example of a very general markup scheme. In contrast, EAD is an extremely specific XML application, providing a standard way of encoding a single type of document. EAD is used for marking up archival finding aids and so has a very direct importance to the library community.

For those who do not frequent archives, archival materials are generally arranged in series of folders in boxes. So, you might have 20 boxes filled with the correspondence of a particular individual, each box containing a number of folders. A researcher wishing to make use of that material would need some guide to tell her where to start looking. These guides are called finding aids, and they can range from being a sort of terse laundry list (folder 1: letters 1945, folder 2: letters 1946) to descriptive works of considerable depth and scholarship. Traditionally, the finding aids are kept in binders in the public area of an archive. More recently, archives have been putting their finding aids up on the Web in HTML but, as we have discussed, this does not provide much flexibility in terms of searching or information retrieval—it really just makes them look nice.

Enter the Encoded Archival Description from the Library of Congress. Like TEI, this was initially an SGML application and it has an important practical lesson to teach us about one of the practical advantages of XML over SGML. When people first got involved in EAD, some archives would put their finding aids on the Web both in HTML and SGML/EAD. Since Web browsers could not read EAD, they would point users to a place where they could download Panorama, a free SGML reader. Panorama was then bought by a company who wanted to charge for it and suddenly there was no free SGML reader anymore. This demonstrates a practical advantage of the greater simplicity of XML relative to SGML. It is *much* easier to write software that parses XML than to write software that parses SGML. In fact, one of the goals of the W3C working group that developed XML was that XML should be simple enough so that a DPH (desperate Perl hacker) could write an XML parser in a weekend. So, it's not likely that libraries will get stuck in the Panorama bind with XML.

The XML incarnation of EAD allows archivists to make their finding aids available in a "smart" format that lets them express concepts specific to archives, concepts like filing units, calendars, physical description, access restrictions, etc. One area where EAD falls down a bit is human readability. From the bad old days of SGML, it has inherited some rather cryptic tags like "dsc" (description of subordinate components) and "add" (adjunct descriptive data). Still, if you use it with any frequency, you'll learn the few odd tags quickly enough.

Remember that EAD is only about marking up the finding aids, not the documents themselves, so it is really a metadata initiative (as implied by the name Encoded Archival *Description*). This seems to be a point of confusion and I often hear people talk about marking up letters or files in EAD. EAD is for marking up one kind of document only: the archival finding aid.

Open Archives Initiative

Note: OAI uses the term "archive" purely in the dictionary sense of a body of stored information, not in the more specific sense that librarians and archivists use the term.

I titled this chapter "Enabling Data Sharing," because I see that as the prime benefit of all the trouble we go to with DTDs and encoding. The next application I'd like to talk about is very much about sharing data, in particular metadata about electronic text archives. OAI is not a markup scheme, so is not really analogous to TEI and EAD. It is a protocol which is designed for "harvesting" XML-encoded metadata that is provided by participants in the project. You can see OAI as the payoff for all the hard work you would do if you were to create an electronic repository of texts. OAI is a protocol that will allow you to communicate your metadata to the world (or at least to other institutions participating in OAI). From the viewpoint of the institution, this means setting up a server that will expose your metadata in a way such that OAI "harvesters" can access the data and make it available to other institutions.

Note that right now the OAI harvests only XML-encoded Dublin Core metadata, so if you have been encoding your metadata in some other form (like TEI headers), you will probably need to use "cross-walks" (i.e. maps that translate from one metadata format to another) to create DC records for your collection if you want to participate in the OAI. There are currently about 100 institutions making metadata available to OAI harvesters.

The OAI represents the kind of thing that got me excited about XML in the first place—the ability to use Internet protocols to share scholarly information in a very controlled and meaningful way.

chapter 4

Stylesheets for XML

In Chapter 1, I made the statement that XML, being a data format, does not really *do* anything. This was largely to save you from feeling any disappointment when you read through pages of technical material that contains nothing that could qualify as a "gee-whiz" demonstration. What I said is true, but the good news is that there are huge numbers of tools available to do just about anything you want to do with XML-encoded data. I should also note that while XML itself has remained remarkably stable (still on version 1.0 after about five years), the technologies surrounding it are in a constant state of change and growth.

The technologies that are of most interest to beginners in XML are the two flavors of stylesheets that are available for use with XML. These can be used with XML in a way that is really not very different from how you would use them with HTML (in fact, in some respects it is easier). I will cover the use of CSS with XML a little bit, but the bulk of this chapter will be devoted to XSL, a style language that is specific to XML and that will allow you to do a vast number of things with your XML documents, including some of the tricks like sorting and filtering that were demonstrated in the "new books" example in Chapter 2.

CSS for XML

Using CSS with XML is very easy. All you have to do is provide formatting information for the different elements in your markup.

Our example for this section is a marked-up set of entries from the catalog of a rare book dealer:

```
<?xml version="1.0" encoding="UTF-8"?>
<!DOCTYPE rarebooks SYSTEM "rarebooks.dtd">
<rarebooks>
<book inventory_number="A3692" price="4200.00">
```

```
 <author>
<last_name>Acosta</last_name>
        <first_name>Jos&#233; de</first_name>
 </author>
 <title>De natvra Novi Orbis et De promvlgatione Evangelii, apvd barbaros, sive De
procvranda Indorvm salvte libri sex.</title>
 <imprint
place="Salmanti&#230;"
        publisher="Apud Guillelmum Foquel"
        year="1589" />
 <binding>Contemporary limp vellum, ties lacking. Three of the six cover edges variously
gnawed by a neat rodent. Title-page with three early owners' names. Lower outside cor-
ner of title-page perished and restored, slightly affecting imprint area. Same restoration
to same corners of next two leaves without loss of text. Some waterstaining or cockling.
Some sidenote shaved by the binder. Final four leaves of the index with fine paper
repairs in lower margin; some loss of text, especially on final two leaves. A copy in fair
condition, buffeted by the years.</binding>
 <note>This copy has a fair amount of later 17th-century marginalia, chiefly in Spanish,
but some in Latin, commenting on the text, with note of how things have or have not
changed.</note>
</book>
<book inventory_number="B34" price="2800.00">
 <author>
 <last_name>Bonnefons</last_name>
         <first_name>Nicholas de</first_name>
 </author>
 <title>Les delices de la campagne, suitte du jardinier fran&#231;ois, o&#249; est
enseign&#233; &#224; preparer pour l'usage de la vie tout ce qui croist sur la terre,
&amp; dans eles eaux.</title>
 <imprint
place="Amsterdam"
        publisher="Chez Iean Blaev"
        year="1661" />
</book>
<book inventory_number="C588" price="300.00">
 <author>
<last_name>Contarini</last_name>
        <first_name>Gasparo</first_name>
 </author>
 <title>De repvblica Venetorvm libri quinque</title>
 <imprint
place="Lvgd. Batavorvm"
        publisher="Ex officina Elzeviriana"
        year="1628"/>
 <binding>Later pointill&#233; gilt-stamped olive calf, spine gilt extra with floral and
avian devices; all edges gilt. Clasps once present lacking; all somewhat rubbed and
abraded but still very attractive. A very few, very faint spots, pages otherwise clean; two
leaves with lower corners torn away.</binding>
 <note>An early entry in the famous Elzevir Republica series, Contarini's history of the
```

```
Venetian republic is a Renaissance classic that first came into print off the Parisian press
of Michael Vascosan in 1543. The engraved title-page here is a typically attractive Elzevir
effort, containing a title banner, aerial view of Venice, and fruit and vegetable arrange-
ments, all surmounted by a rather smug-looking winged lion possessively clutching an
open book.</note>
</book>
<book inventory_number="C2739" price="8500.00">
 <author>
 <last_name>Cort&#233;s</last_name>
 <first_name>Hernando</first_name>
 </author>
 <title>La preclara narratione di Ferdinando Cortese della Nuoua Hispagna del Mare
Oceano</title>
 <imprint
place="Venetia"
        publisher="Bernardino de Viano . . . ad instantia de Baptista de Pederzani"
        year="1582"/>
 <binding>Later limp mottled calf. Large and handsome red wax seal of the Cardinals of
Hungary on the title-page, overlapping an elaborately detailed woodcut border. The vol-
ume now well housed in a half green morocco and cloth case.</binding>
</book>
<book inventory_number="H442" price="3750.00">
 <author>
<last_name>Hotman</last_name>
        <first_name>Fran&#231;ois</first_name>
 </author>
 <title>Francogallia</title>
 <imprint
place="Genev&#230;"
        publisher="Ex officina Stoerii"
        year="1573"/>
 <binding>Contemporary limp vellum. Paper shelf label on spine. A library's blind pres-
sure-stamps; properly deaccessioned with no additional stamps. A really nice
copy.</binding>
</book>
<book inventory_number="P4568" price="8500.00">
 <author>
<last_name>Petrarca</last_name>
        <first_name>Francesco</first_name>
 </author>
 <title>De los remedios contra p[ro]spera y aduersa fortuna</title>
 <imprint
place="Sevilla"
        publisher="Jacobo Cromberger"
        year="1513"/>
 <binding>Later reverse calf (suede).</binding>
 <note>With the bookplate of the enigmatic Cuban book collector, Oscar Cintas.</note>
</book>
</rarebooks>
```

In figure 15 we see the document presented in IE's ugly default mode.

Obviously, we would never want to inflict this on the public. At this point, remember, we have not given IE any information about how we want our various elements to be displayed, so it applies a generic rule for the display of elements.

So, let's write a simple stylesheet that just says that we'd like to see the title of each book in bold. All we have to say is:

title {font-weight:bold;}

We'll save this single line of text in a file called simple.css. We would link the document to this stylesheet by inserting a PI after the XML declaration:

<?xml-stylesheet type="text/css" href="simple.css"?>

CSS is probably the easiest Web-related technology out there. All you do is list the various elements of your document and provide formatting rules for each. The only thing at all difficult is remembering what the various properties are called (for instance remembering that bold is a font-weight, not a font-style). There are various cheat sheets available on the Web to help with this: one good one is from Webmonkey (http://hotwired.lycos.com/webmonkey/reference/stylesheet_guide/css_properties.html).

In figure 16, we now see a flat dump of the document content (since we have provided a stylesheet, IE stops trying to apply its defaults). This is still ugly, but you'll notice that the titles are indeed bold.

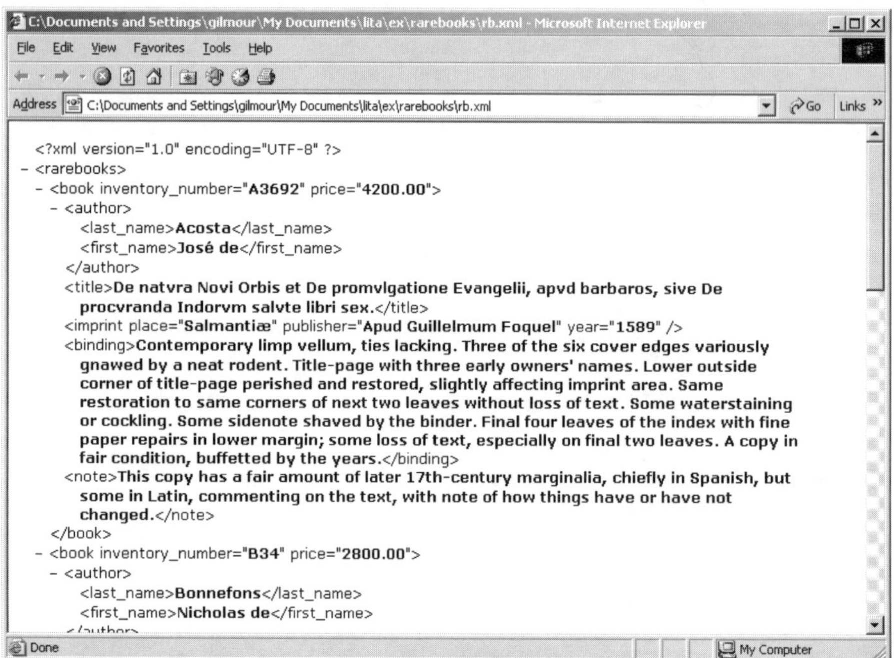

```
C:\Documents and Settings\gilmour\My Documents\lita\ex\rarebooks\rb.xml - Microsoft Internet Explorer
File  Edit  View  Favorites  Tools  Help
Address  C:\Documents and Settings\gilmour\My Documents\lita\ex\rarebooks\rb.xml   Go  Links

  <?xml version="1.0" encoding="UTF-8" ?>
- <rarebooks>
  - <book inventory_number="A3692" price="4200.00">
    - <author>
        <last_name>Acosta</last_name>
        <first_name>José de</first_name>
      </author>
      <title>De natvra Novi Orbis et De promvlgatione Evangelii, apvd barbaros, sive De
        procvranda Indorvm salvte libri sex.</title>
      <imprint place="Salmantiæ" publisher="Apud Guillelmum Foquel" year="1589" />
      <binding>Contemporary limp vellum, ties lacking. Three of the six cover edges variously
        gnawed by a neat rodent. Title-page with three early owners' names. Lower outside
        corner of title-page perished and restored, slightly affecting imprint area. Same
        restoration to same corners of next two leaves without loss of text. Some waterstaining
        or cockling. Some sidenote shaved by the binder. Final four leaves of the index with fine
        paper repairs in lower margin; some loss of text, especially on final two leaves. A copy in
        fair condition, buffetted by the years.</binding>
      <note>This copy has a fair amount of later 17th-century marginalia, chiefly in Spanish, but
        some in Latin, commenting on the text, with note of how things have or have not
        changed.</note>
    </book>
  - <book inventory_number="B34" price="2800.00">
    - <author>
        <last_name>Bonnefons</last_name>
        <first_name>Nicholas de</first_name>
Done                                                         My Computer
```

figure 15: The rare books list displayed in Internet Explorer's default mode.

By adding a few more rules, we can make the document a bit prettier:

```
book, author, title, binding, note {
 display: block;
 font-family: Garamond, serif;
}
book {
 margin-bottom:2em;
 margin-left:2em;
 margin-right:2em;
}
author {
 color: red;
 font-size: 1.3em;
 font-weight: bold;
}
title {
 font-size: 1.3em;
 font-style: italic;
 font-weight: bold;
}
title:first-letter {
 font-size: 1.5em;
}
```

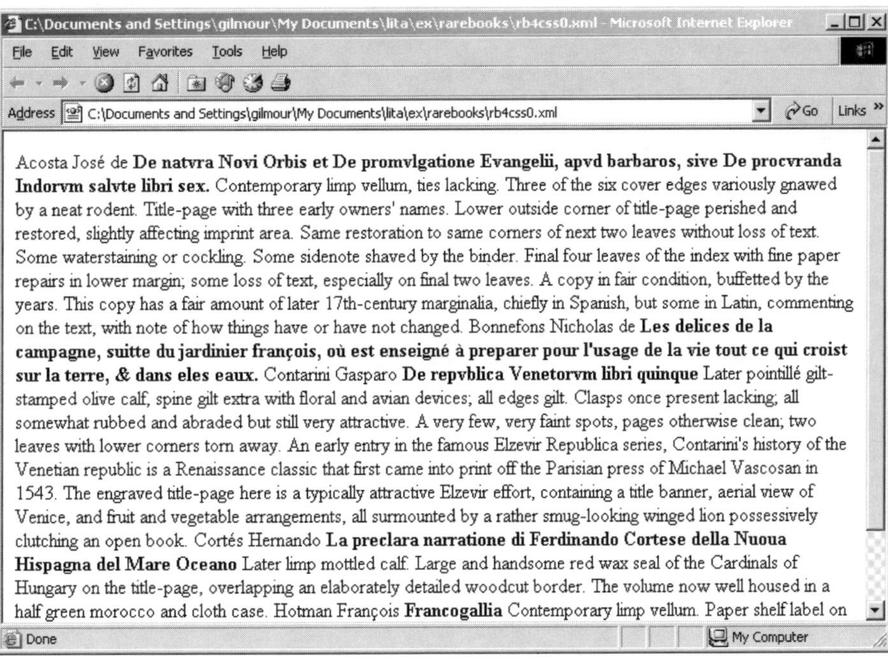

figure 16: The rare books list displayed with a simple CSS stylesheet.

The stylesheet in figure 17 mostly adjusts margins and various font properties. Yet another CSS stylesheet on the same document:

```
book, author, title, binding, note {
 display: block;
 margin-left:2cm;
        margin-right:2cm;
}
author, title, binding, note {
 font-family: Verdana, sans-serif;
}
author {
 margin-top:1em;
 background-color: #006699;
 color: yellow;
 font-size: 2em;
}
title {
 font-family: serif;
 font-weight: bold;
 font-style: italic;
 font-variant: small-caps;
 font-size: 1.3em;
}
```


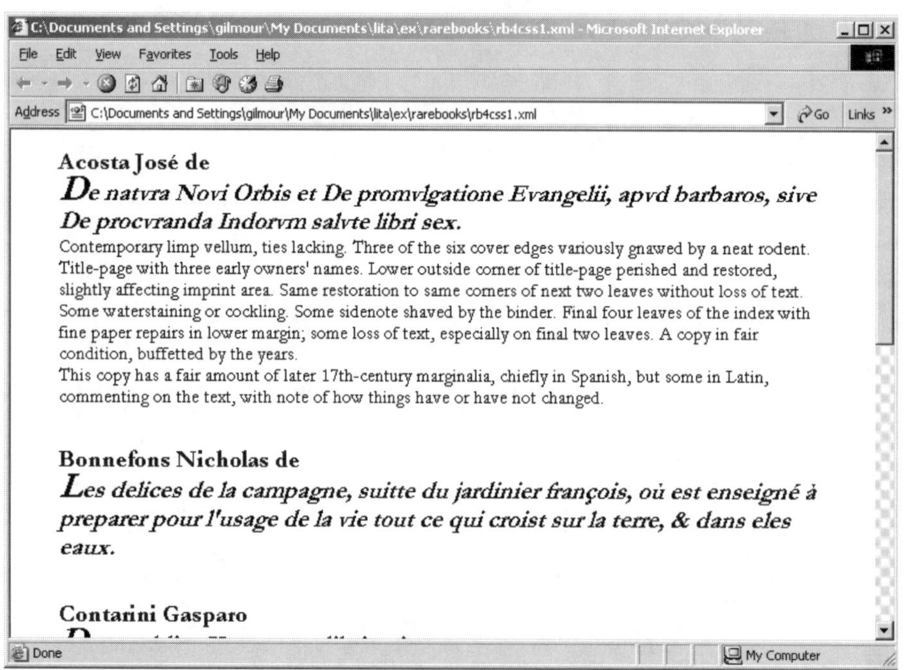

figure 17: The rare books list displayed with a more complex CSS stylesheet.

This produces the appearance shown in figure 18.

In this case I have also adjusted the background-color property on the author names to make them appear as dark blue banners. This is a handy trick if you want to avoid making little gif files for text labels for your Web pages.

You will notice that a lot of information from the original document is conspicuously missing from all the examples I have shown with CSS. Price, inventory number, and all the imprint information are nowhere to be seen. In the original XML document, these are encoded as attributes. This is one of the many weaknesses of CSS—it will not display attribute values. Add that to your list of things to consider when deciding whether to encode something as a child element or an attribute. (And to your list of things to think about when deciding between CSS and XSL.)

I haven't devoted many pages to CSS because I believe that for the most part it isn't worth the trouble. (Also, by now, most HTML authors are familiar with CSS anyway.) If you have an XML document that you want to display more or less as-is and you just want it to look nice, then CSS is fine. If you want anything more complicated than that, you should think about XSL.

XSL

Sometimes I think that XSL (Extensible Stylesheet Language) is almost a misnomer. It especially seems that way if the only style language that you are familiar with is CSS.

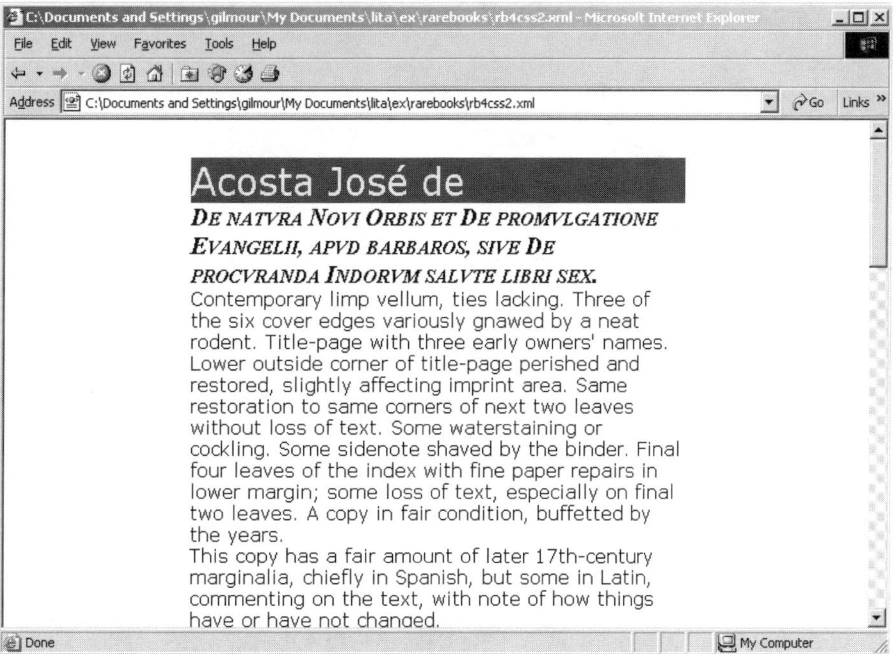

figure 18: The rare books list displayed with a third CSS stylesheet.

While CSS allows the styling of individual elements, XSL is actually a sort of limited programming language for transforming XML documents in addition to a means of providing what we normally think of as style information (fonts, colors, margins, etc.).

XSL is actually a three-part technology. The first part is properly called XSLT (XSL Transformations), which is the main thing that I will cover here. The second part is called XPath, which is an expression language for addressing particular parts of an XML document. The third part is XSLFO (XSL Formatting Objects), which is the part of XSL that deals with issues of layout and typography, but in ways which are much more specific than CSS.

One interesting thing about XSL is that it is actually a flavor of XML, so an XSL stylesheet is a well-formed XML document in itself. (Note that this makes it much easier to write software for XSL, since if you have an XML parser, you're already halfway there.)

XSLT is used for transforming XML documents into another format. Perhaps the most common application is to transform XML to HTML (or XHTML), but it can also be used for XML to XML conversions (say, to implement a crosswalk between two XML-based metadata formats), XML to PDF, XML to plain text, etc.

Let's take a look at an example of a simple XML to HTML transformation.

```
<?xml version="1.0" encoding="UTF-8"?>
<xsl:stylesheet version="1.0" xmlns:xsl="www.w3.org/1999/XSL/Transform">
<!–First template: matches the document root and
 creates the high-level html tags. –>
 <xsl:template match="/">
 <html>
 <body>
 <h1>Some Rare Books</h1>
 <xsl:apply-templates/>
 </body>
 </html>
 </xsl:template>
<!–Second template: matches book elements and outputs
 their titles as second-level headers. –>
 <xsl:template match="book">
 <p>
 <h2><xsl:value-of select="title"/></h2>
 <hr/>
 </p>
 </xsl:template>
</xsl:stylesheet>
```

This stylesheet causes produces an HTML document that looks like figure 19.

Only the titles of the books are displayed, each of them as an HTML "h2" element.

Try not to be put off by the fairly complex syntax of XSL. XSL stylesheets are notorious, even among seasoned programmers, for being ugly, but they actually have a simple, regular structure that makes them not all that bad once you're used to them.

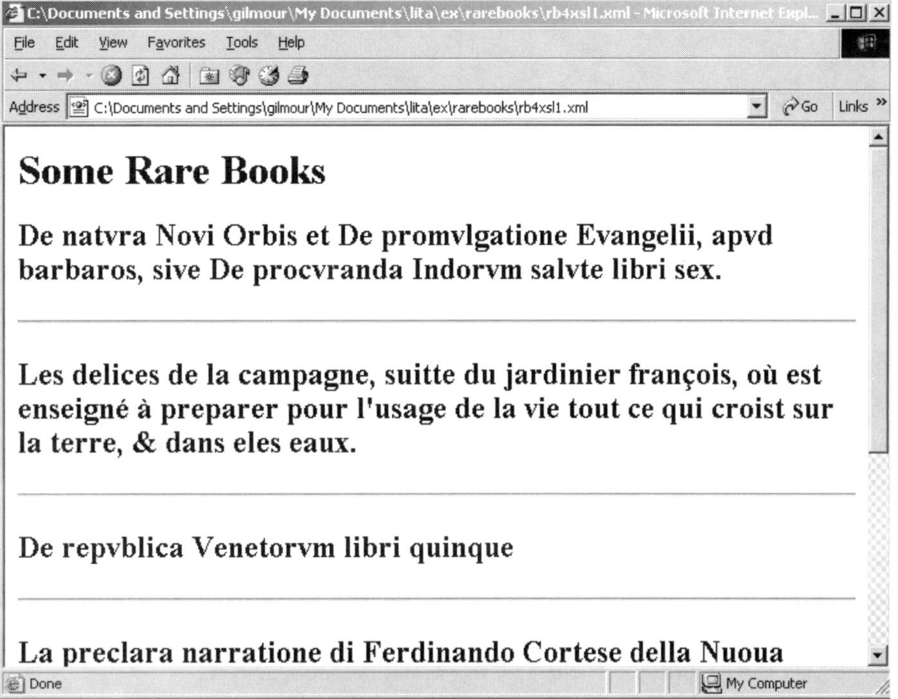

figure 19: The rare books list displayed with a simple XSL stylesheet that displays only the titles.

The above stylesheet really only contains four basic things: an XML declaration (remember, it is a well-formed XML document), a root element called "xsl:stylesheet" (which is the same for all XSL stylesheets), and two templates.

Any XSL file will contain a single root element called "xsl:stylesheet," which usually looks like this:

```
<xsl:stylesheet version="1.0" xmlns:xsl="www.w3.org/1999/XSL/Transform">
```

The colons that you see here refer to things called namespaces. Think of namespaces as labels for the elements belonging to a particular application. The way that we give labels to things on the Web is by using a URI (Uniform Resource Identifier, a more generalized case of the familiar URL or Web address). But since URIs can be very lengthy, we designate a shorthand for the URI with which we want to label our elements. All of the tags used in XSL are defined as being part of the XSL namespace, so they all start with "xsl:". The "xmlns:xsl" attribute defines the actual URI for which we are substituting the abbreviation "xsl."

The "xsl:stylesheet" element contains a series of templates, each enclosed in an element called "xsl:template." Remember this: no matter how ugly a stylesheet looks, it is just a series of templates and if you break it down in your mind into those basic units it won't seem so bad. A template as a set of instructions indicating what the XSL processor should do when it encounters a particular element. Let's look at the first template of our stylesheet:

```
<xsl:template match="/">
 <html>
 <body>
 <h1>Some Rare Books</h1>
 <xsl:apply-templates/>
 </body>
 </html>
</xsl:template>
```

The "match" attribute of the "xsl:template" element tells us what element to apply this template to. The forward slash refers to the document root, which can be thought of as a hypothetical "super-element" that is the parent of the XML document's root element. Think of this as matching the document itself.

So, if we translate this template into English, it says: "When you encounter the document, produce an 'html' element that should include a 'body' element. The body element should include an "h1" element with the textual content 'Some Rare Books.' After you've done that, see if there are any more templates to apply. If so, put the output from those templates after the 'h1' element, but within the 'body' element."

That last part again: think of the "xsl:apply-templates" element as saying "continue working here" or "whatever else you have to do, do it here."

Now, the second template:


```
<xsl:template match="book">
 <p>
 <h2><xsl:value-of select="title"/></h2>
 <hr/>
 </p>
</xsl:template>
```

This template matches the book element. Translated into English, the template says: "When you encounter any book element, create a 'p' element. The 'p' element should have two children: the first an 'h2' element containing the book's title, and the second an empty 'hr' element." (Note that, contrary to our HTML instincts, we have to make sure the "hr" is closed, otherwise your stylesheet wouldn't be a well-formed XML document).

The "xsl:value-of" element is the one that you will use most often for actually inserting data into the result of the transformation. It takes a "select" attribute that tells the processor what precise bit of information you want inserted.

So, the output of this transformation is an HTML document:

```
<html>
<body>
<h1>Some Rare Books</h1>
<p>
```

```
<h2>De natvra Novi Orbis ...</h2>
</p>
<hr/>
<p>
<h2>Les delices de la campagne ...</h2>
</p>
<hr/>
...
</body>
</html>
```

Incidentally, IE automatically renders the HTML for display when you're using a stylesheet that converts to HTML. If you try to "View Source" normally, you'll just see the XML document. If you want to actually see the HTML code that is produced (which can be very helpful for de-bugging), you'll need to download the IE XML Tools that were mentioned earlier. In addition to the "Validate XML" option, installing this package also adds a "View XSL Output" choice to the right-click menu, which will show you the actual HTML code produced by the transformation.

Let's move on to a more complex example. This stylesheet produces a table showing the author's last name, title, year of publication, and price.

```
<?xml version="1.0" encoding="UTF-8"?>
<xsl:stylesheet version="1.0" xmlns:xsl="www.w3.org/1999/XSL/Transform">
<!–First template: matches the root element and
 creates the high-level html tags. Note that a
 CSS style section is included in the head element. –>
 <xsl:template match="/">
 <html>
 <head>
 <style type="text/css">
 body {font-family: Garamond, serif;}
 table {border-width: medium; border-style: solid;}
 td {border-width: thin; border-style:solid; padding:0.5em;}
 td.title {font-style: italic;}
 </style>
 </head>
 <body>
 <h1>Some Rare Books</h1>
 <table>
 <xsl:apply-templates select="rarebooks/book">
 <xsl:sort data-type="number" select="imprint/@year"/>
 </xsl:apply-templates>
 </table>
 </body>
 </html>
 </xsl:template>
<!–Second template: matches book elements –>
 <xsl:template match="book">
```

```
<tr>
<td><xsl:value-of select="author/last_name"/></td>
<td class="title"><xsl:value-of select="title"/></td>
<td><xsl:value-of select="imprint/@year"/></td>
<td>$<xsl:value-of select="@price"/></td>
</tr>
</xsl:template>
</xsl:stylesheet>
```

This stylesheet still only contains two templates. As in the previous example, the first template matches the document root. Here, I have included a head, which should contain a <style> element with CSS style information. This is one of the nice things about using XSLT to produce HTML output–for style information you can just use the same old tricks that you already know for HTML; there's no reason to worry about the much more complicated XSLFO.

After the head, there is of course a body, which again contains a level 1 header. This is followed by a <table> element, into which we insert the content using an "xsl:apply-templates" element. Unlike the previous example, this element is here provided with a "select" attribute to explicitly state which elements these rules will apply to. This example is a little unusual in that the normally empty "xsl:apply-templates" element isn't empty, but contains a child called "xsl:sort," which does exactly what you would think. You specify the field that you want to sort on using the "select" attribute and the nature of the sorting using the "data-type" attribute. If you want to provide a second sort key, you can do that by making a second "xsl:sort" element as a child of "xsl:apply-templates."

Notice the value of the "select" attributes in this example, both on the "xsl:apply-templates" and "xsl:sort." The values of these attributes are examples of XPath expressions. Remember that XPath is the part of XSL that allows you to address particular parts of an XML document.

The expression "imprint/@year" means to sort on the value of the year attribute (the "@" indicates that it is an attribute) of the <imprint> element. The XPath expression must start from whatever the current template is matching, in this case "book."

Now the second template of the stylesheet:

```
<xsl:template match="book">
<tr>
<td><xsl:value-of select="author/last_name"/></td>
<td class="title"><xsl:value-of select="title"/></td>
<td><xsl:value-of select="imprint/@year"/></td>
<td>$<xsl:value-of select="@price"/></td>
</tr>
</xsl:template>
```

This template matches <book> elements. For each book element, it produces a "tr" (table row) element, containing four cells, each with a particular bit of information as indicated by an XPath expression in the "select" attribute of the "xsl:value-of" element. So, the result of this transformation is a sorted, tabular layout of the book information (see figure 20). The formatting of the titles in italic is controlled by the CSS section included in the XSL stylesheet.

Currently, IE is the only browser that supports XSL. This means, of course, that you cannot rely on client-side support for the use of XSL. If you want to use XSL on the Web, you will need to make use of some type of server-side processing in which your server prepares data that can be read by any browsers your users may have on their computers. The optimal route is to use a ready-made XML publishing environment such as Cocoon, available from the Apache XML Project (http://xml.apache.org). If this is not an option for you (for instance, if you're not running your own server), you can use an XSL processor on your desktop to produce HTML documents that you can then make available on your Web site.

Still, IE provides a readily available testbed where you can freely experiment with XSL, so I encourage students to use it while they're learning. Microsoft was actually a very early adopter of XSL. In fact, with IE5 they were a little too early, basing their support on a working draft of the XSL standard. Following the release of IE5, XSL underwent some drastic changes, resulting in an unfortunate situation in which you could either write good, W3C-compliant XSL or XSL that would work in a real browser. Thankfully, this has improved with IE6, so we can finally write XSL that works with IE and with other tools. For this reason I strongly recommend that if you want to play with XSL at home you use IE6. The examples in this book will not work in IE5.x.

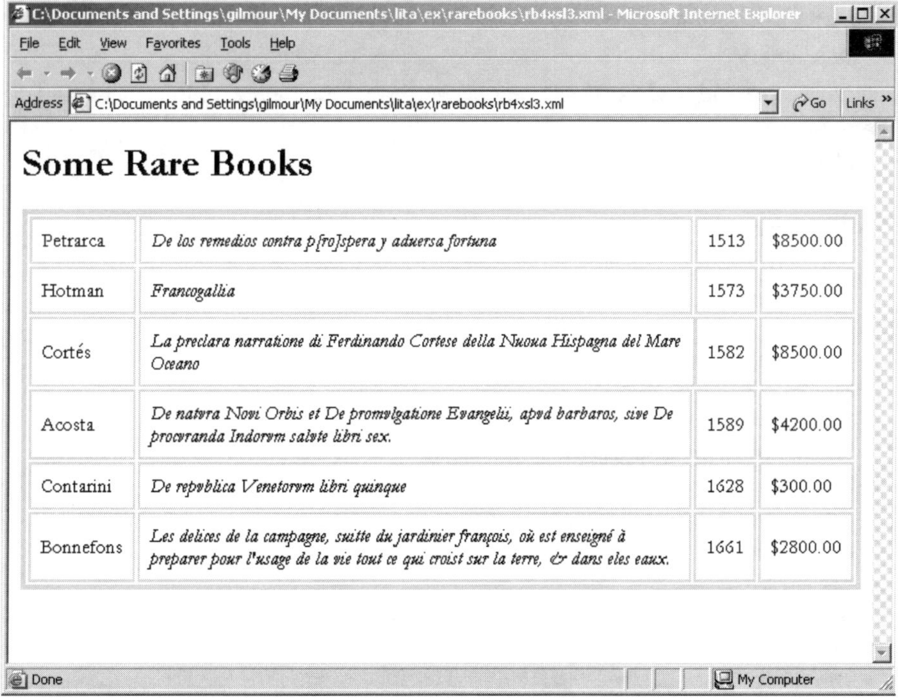

Some Rare Books

Petrarca	*De los remedios contra p[ro]spera y aduersa fortuna*	1513	$8500.00
Hotman	*Francogallia*	1573	$3750.00
Cortés	*La preclara narratione di Ferdinando Cortese della Nuoua Hispagna del Mare Oceano*	1582	$8500.00
Acosta	*De natvra Novi Orbis et De promvlgatione Evangelii, apvd barbaros, sive De procvranda Indorvm salvte libri sex.*	1589	$4200.00
Contarini	*De repvblica Venetorvm libri quinque*	1628	$300.00
Bonnefons	*Les delices de la campagne, suitte du jardinier françois, où est enseigné à preparer pour l'usage de la vie tout ce qui croist sur la terre, & dans les eaux.*	1661	$2800.00

figure 20: Data from the rare books list displayed selectively, in tabular form, using an XSL stylesheet.

One situation in which XML really shines is when you have information that you need to make available in various formats. One such example that we come across in libraries is the time-honored reference handout. Since the advent of the Web, of course, these things are now mostly online, but we nevertheless pay homage to our professional ancestry by stocking kiosks in the reference area with paper copies of these guides that patrons can take with them. Of course in our current environment of rapid change, we have to frequently update these documents. Wouldn't it be nice if we could update them once and then produce either Web pages or handouts as needed? XML allows us to do just that, making possible a number of different transformations.

Many people think that the "next big thing" in terms of Web technology will be web-enabled cell phones and PDAs, so one might also want to write stylesheets that would produce WML versions of the pages. Another interesting possibility is linking stylesheets to software that detects the visitor's browser, so that different flavors of HTML may be produced depending on the brand and release of the user's browser. This is nice in that it allows the webmaster to take advantage of all the nifty features offered by newer browsers without fear that he or she is excluding those visitors still using Netscape 3. Note that IE does not include any support for XSLFO, so the documents you see here were all produced using the free tools provided by the Apache XML Project (Xerces, Xalan, and FOP). This is all free, Java-based software available from xml.apache.org.

The following demonstration shows how we can use XSLT and XSLFO to create two different formats of the same information. When I worked at the University at Albany's Science Library, we had a number of subject guides that were kept both in kiosks in the reference area and made available on our Web site. I took a few of these and marked them up in XML.

This is the guide for chemistry:

```
<?xml version="1.0" encoding="UTF-8"?>
<!DOCTYPE research_guide SYSTEM "ResearchGuides.dtd">
<research_guide>
<meta>
<Title>Chemistry: A Brief Guide to Reference Resources</Title>
<Date>2000-11-08</Date>
<Language>en</Language>
<Subject>chemistry</Subject>
<Relation>www.albany.edu/library/virtual/subject/chem.htm</Relation>
<Creator email="gilmr@albany.edu">Ron Gilmour</Creator>
</meta>
<section ID="glit">
<section_title>Guides to the Literature</section_title>
<entry><entry_title>How to Find Chemical Information, by Robert E. Maizell</entry_title>
<callnumber>SCIENCE REF QD 8.5 M34 1998</callnumber>
<annotation>Thorough, up to date treatment on the use of chemical information sources.
Includes chapters on Chemical Abstracts, Beilstein, and Gmelin.</annotation></entry>
</section>
<section ID="data">
```

```
<section_title>Databases, Indexes and Abstracts</section_title>
<entry><entry_title>Chemical Abstracts</entry_title>
<callnumber>SCIENCE REF / Index QD 1 A51</callnumber>
<annotation>The definitive bibliographic resource for all fields of chemistry, dating back
to 1907. Indexes both the journal and patent literature. The University at Albany has lim-
ited electronic access to the CA databases. Inquire at the Science Library reference desk
for information on electronic searching. See Maizell's How to Find Chemical Information
<callnumber>SCIENCE REF QD 8.5 M34 1998</callnumber> or CAS Printed Access
Tools: A User Guide <callnumber>SCIENCE QD 9 C37 1984</callnumber> for assis-
tance with the paper CA.</annotation></entry>
<entry><entry_title>Science Citation Index</entry_title>
<callnumber>SCIENCE REF / Index Q 1 Z999 S28</callnumber>
<annotation>Produced by the Institute for Scientific Information, this indexes the core
journals in chemistry (about 250 titles). Searchable by author, title keyword, author's
address, or by cited reference which links current and past publications. The Science
Library has 1964+ ; also available in CD-ROM format (1980+). Request the CD-ROMs at
the Science Circulation Desk.</annotation></entry>
</section>
<section ID=“dict”>
<section_title>Dictionaries and Encyclopedias</section_title>
<entry><entry_title>Comprehensive Organic Chemistry</entry_title>
<callnumber>SCIENCE REF QD 245 C65</callnumber>
<annotation>This six volume encyclopedic reference is organized topically rather than
alphabetically, but volume 6 provides a detailed index.</annotation></entry>
<entry><entry_title>Dictionary of Organic Compounds</entry_title>
<callnumber>SCIENCE REF QD 246 D5 1996</callnumber>
<annotation>Alphabetical listing of organic compounds providing basic physical and
chemical properties and bibliographic references. Nine volumes, of which the first six are
content. Volumes seven through nine are indexes by name, molecular formula, and CAS
Registry number, respectively.</annotation></entry>
<entry><entry_title>Dictionary of Organometallic Compounds</entry_title>
<callnumber>SCIENCE REF QD 411 D53 1984</callnumber>
<annotation>Similar to the Dictionary of Organic Compounds in layout and organization.
Arranged alphabetically by the name of the metallic component of the compound. Two
volumes (plus a third index volume) constitute the original work. Five supplementary vol-
umes and a cumulative index have been produced since.</annotation></entry>
<entry><entry_title>Kirk-Othmer Encyclopedia of Chemical Technology</entry_title>
<callnumber>SCIENCE REF TP 9 E685</callnumber>
<annotation>Multivolume encyclopedia covering all aspects of applied chemistry. Articles
are generally very readable and accessible to the non-specialist.</annotation></entry>
<entry><entry_title>Macmillan Encyclopedia of Chemistry</entry_title>
<callnumber>SCIENCE REF QD 4 M33 1997</callnumber>
<annotation>Excellent source for introductory information on chemical subjects. Four
volume set containing signed articles with bibliographies.</annotation></entry>
</section>
<section ID=“biog”>
<section_title>Biography</section_title>
<entry><entry_title>The Biographical Dictonary of Scientists: Chemists</entry_title>
<callnumber>SCIENCE REF QD 21 B48 1983B</callnumber>
```

```
<annotation>Contains biographies of chemists and a short historical
introduction.</annotation></entry>
<entry><entry_title>Dictionary of Scientific Biography</entry_title>
<callnumber>SCIENCE REF Q 141 D5</callnumber>
<annotation>Multi-volume encyclopedia containing essays on scientists from all periods
of history. Each essay is signed by the contributor and includes a bibliography. 14 vol-
umes plus indexes and supplements.</annotation></entry>
<entry><entry_title>Notable Twentieth-Century Scientists</entry_title>
<callnumber>SCIENCE REF Q 141 N73 1995</callnumber>
<annotation>This four-volume set is a comprehensive source of biographical information
on over 1,300 scientists active in the 20th century. Each biographical entry includes a 2
or 3 page essay, a list of selected writings, and a bibliography. There are field of special-
ization, gender, nationality/ethnicity, and subject indexes.</annotation></entry>
</section>
<section ID="hand">
<section_title>Handbooks and Compendiums</section_title>
<entry><entry_title>Beilsteins Handbuch der organischen Chemie</entry_title>
<callnumber>SCIENCE REF / Index QD 251 B4 1918</callnumber>
<annotation>The essential source for information on organic compounds, including
properties and bibliographic references. Organized into an original series (H) and five
supplementary series (E I - E V). Each series has its own index volumes, both to molecu-
lar formulas (formelregister) and to subjects (sachsregister). A cummulative index
(Gesamtregister) was produced following the fourth series. See How to Use Beilstein
<callnumber>SCIENCE REF QD 251 B42x</callnumber> for assistance with this com-
plex resource.</annotation></entry>
<entry><entry_title>CRC Handbook of Chemistry and Physics</entry_title>
<callnumber>SCIENCE REF QD 65 H3</callnumber>
<annotation>The classic ready-reference book of physical and chemical data. It is issued
annually with revised information and new material. Previous editions are available in the
Science Library's circulating collection.</annotation></entry>
<entry><entry_title>Gmelins Handbuch der anorganischen Chemie</entry_title>
<callnumber>SCIENCE REF / Index QD 151 G52</callnumber>
<annotation>The inorganic chemistry analog to Beilstein, providing chemical information
on inorganic compounds. The volumes are organized by "system numbers," with anion-
forming elements having the lower numbers and cation-forming elements having the
higher numbers. To aid the researcher, the element symbols are marked on yellow cards
which are placed between the volumes. See Maizell's How to Find Chemical Information
<callnumber>SCIENCE REF QD 8.5 M34 1998</callnumber> for help with this
resource.</annotation></entry>
</section>
<section ID="curr">
<section_title>Current Awareness Service</section_title>
<entry><entry_title>UnCover Reveal</entry_title>
<url accessibility="UAOnly">http://uncweb.carl.org/reveal/</url>
<annotation>An automated current awareness service that delivers the tables of contents
of journals, citations, and books by electronic mail. Search strategies can also be created
by word or author. Instructions on how to set up a profile are available at the UnCover
Reveal site.</annotation></entry>
</section>
```

```
</research_guide>
```

I wrote two stylesheets. The first transformed the XML source into HTML for the web:

```
<?xml version=“1.0” encoding=“UTF-8”?>
<xsl:stylesheet xmlns:xsl=“www.w3.org/1999/XSL/Transform” version=“1.0”>
<!–ROOT TEMPLATE –>
<xsl:template match=“/”>
 <html>
 <head>
 <title>
 <xsl:value-of select=“//meta/Title”/>
 </title>
 <xsl:call-template name=“metadata”/>
 <style>
 body {background-color:#ffffff; font-family:serif;}
 .title {font-weight:bold; font-style:italic;}
 .annotation {margin-left:4em; margin-right:2em;}
 .green {background-color:#f0fff0;
 width:25em;
 border-width:medium;
 border-style:double;
 padding:2em;
 text-align:center;
 margin-top:1.5em;
 margin-bottom:1.5em;}
 p {margin-left:4em; margin-right:2em;}
 h2 {margin-left:2em;}
 </style>
 </head>
 <body>
 <div align=“center”>
 <img alt=“University at Albany Libraries” src=“smallogo.jpg” width=“547” height=“40” />
 <br />
 <h1>
 <xsl:value-of select=“//meta/Title”/>
 </h1>
 </div>
<!–This part creates the internal “quick navigation” links at the top of the page. A link is
created for each “section” element, with the section name as the target text and the sec-
tion ID (prefixed by a pound sign) as the “href”.–>
 <div align=“center”>
 <div style=“margin-left:2em;”>
 <xsl:for-each select=“//section”>
 [<a href=“#{@ID}”><xsl:value-of select=“section_title”/></a>] 
 </xsl:for-each>
 </div>
 </div>
 <hr />
 <xsl:apply-templates select=“//section”/>
 <div style=“text-align:center;align:center”>
```

```
<div class="green">For Web-based resources see the
<xsl:element name="a">
<xsl:attribute name="href">
<xsl:value-of select="//meta/Relation"/>
</xsl:attribute>Subject Guide
</xsl:element>
</div>
</div>
<div>This page maintained by
<xsl:value-of select="research_guide/meta/Creator"/>.
</div>
<div>Comments to
<xsl:element name="a">
<xsl:attribute name="href">
<xsl:value-of select="research_guide/meta/Creator/@email"/>
</xsl:attribute>
<xsl:value-of select="research_guide/meta/Creator/@email"/>
</xsl:element>
.</div>
</body>
</html>
</xsl:template>
<!—SECTION TEMPLATE —>
<xsl:template match="//section">
<h2>
<xsl:element name="a">
<xsl:attribute name="name">
<xsl:value-of select="@ID"/>
</xsl:attribute>
<xsl:value-of select="section_title"/>
</xsl:element>
</h2>
<xsl:apply-templates select="entry"/>
<hr width="50%" />
</xsl:template>
<!—ENTRY TEMPLATE —>
<xsl:template match="//entry">
<p>
<xsl:choose>
<xsl:when test="./url">
<span class="entry_title">
<xsl:element name="a">
<xsl:attribute name="href">
<xsl:value-of select="url"/>
</xsl:attribute>
<xsl:value-of select="entry_title"/>
</xsl:element>
</span>
<xsl:if test="./url[@accessibility='UAOnly']">
```

```
  
<a href="/databases/proxy.html">
<img alt="Accessible to University at Albany users only" width="23" height="15" bor-
der="0" src="ua.gif" />
</a>
</xsl:if>
</xsl:when>
<xsl:otherwise>
<span class="title">
<xsl:value-of select="entry_title"/>
</span>
</xsl:otherwise>
</xsl:choose>
<xsl:if test="./callnumber">
[<xsl:value-of select="callnumber"/>]
</xsl:if>
<div class="annotation">
<xsl:value-of select="annotation"/>
</div>
</p>
</xsl:template>
<!—METADATA TEMPLATE —>
<xsl:template match="meta" name="metadata">
<xsl:element name="meta">
<xsl:attribute name="name">Creator</xsl:attribute>
<xsl:attribute name="content">
<xsl:value-of select="//meta/Creator"/>
</xsl:attribute>
</xsl:element>
<xsl:element name="meta">
<xsl:attribute name="name">Date</xsl:attribute>
<xsl:attribute name="content">
<xsl:value-of select="//meta/Date"/>
</xsl:attribute>
</xsl:element>
<xsl:element name="meta">
<xsl:attribute name="name">Subject</xsl:attribute>
<xsl:attribute name="content">
<xsl:value-of select="//meta/Subject"/>
</xsl:attribute>
</xsl:element>
<xsl:element name="meta">
<xsl:attribute name="name">Language</xsl:attribute>
<xsl:attribute name="content">
<xsl:value-of select="//meta/Language"/>
</xsl:attribute>
</xsl:element>
</xsl:template>
</xsl:stylesheet>
```

This stylesheet produces a Web page that looks like figure 21.

I wrote this second stylesheet that converts the XML file to a PDF document:

```
<?xml version="1.0" encoding="UTF-8"?>
<xsl:stylesheet version="1.0"
xmlns:fo="www.w3.org/1999/XSL/Format"
xmlns:xsl="www.w3.org/1999/XSL/Transform">
<xsl:template match="/">
 <fo:root>
 <fo:layout-master-set>
 <fo:simple-page-master master-name="master"
 page-height="11in"        page-width="8.5in"
 margin-top="1in"          margin-bottom="1in"
 margin-left="1in"         margin-right="1in">
 <fo:region-body/>
 </fo:simple-page-master>
 </fo:layout-master-set>
 <fo:page-sequence master-reference="master">
 <fo:flow flow-name="xsl-region-body">
 <fo:block>
 <fo:table border-width="2pt" background-color="teal">
 <fo:table-column column-width="150pt"/>
```

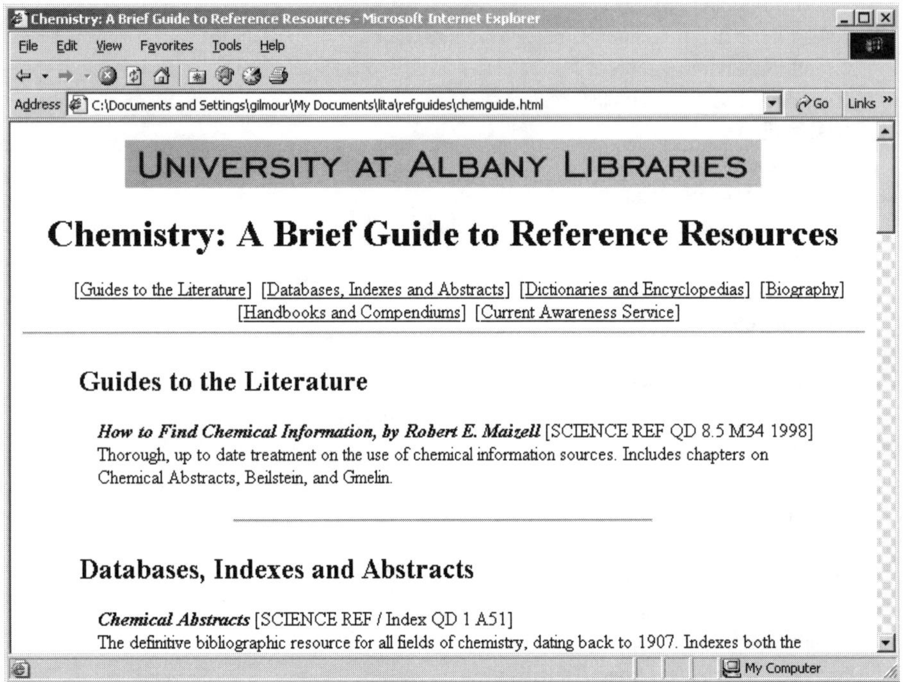

figure 21: Result of transforming a subject guide XML document into HTML using an XSL stylesheet.

```
<fo:table-column column-width="300pt"/>
<fo:table-body>
<fo:table-row>
<fo:table-cell>
 <fo:block>
 <fo:external-graphic src="file:newlibfront.gif"/>
 </fo:block>
</fo:table-cell>
<fo:table-cell padding-left="12pt" padding-top="4pt">
 <fo:block font-size="30pt" color="white"
font-family="sans-serif" line-height="36pt">
 <xsl:value-of select="/research_guide/meta/Title"/>
 </fo:block>
</fo:table-cell>
</fo:table-row>
</fo:table-body>
</fo:table>
</fo:block>
<fo:block text-align="center">
<fo:leader leader-pattern="rule" leader-length="6in" rule-thickness="3pt"/>
</fo:block>
<fo:block border-start-width="2px" border-start-color="black">
<xsl:apply-templates/>
</fo:block>
</fo:flow>
</fo:page-sequence>
</fo:root>
</xsl:template>
<xsl:template match="//meta"/>
<xsl:template match="//section">
 <fo:block>
 <fo:block font-size="14pt" font-family="sans-serif" space-before.optimum="24pt"
space-after.optimum="12pt">
 <xsl:value-of select="section_title"/>
 </fo:block>
 <xsl:apply-templates select="entry"/>
 </fo:block>
</xsl:template>
<xsl:template match="//entry">
 <fo:block space-after.optimum="10pt">
 <fo:block font-size="12pt" font-family="serif">
 <fo:inline font-style="italic" font-weight="bold">
 <xsl:value-of select="entry_title"/>
 <xsl:text>  </xsl:text>
 </fo:inline>
 <xsl:if test="./callnumber">
 <xsl:text>[</xsl:text>
 <xsl:value-of select="callnumber"/>
 <xsl:text>]</xsl:text>
```

```
</xsl:if>
<xsl:if test=“./url”>
<xsl:text>&lt;</xsl:text>
<xsl:value-of select=“url”/>
<xsl:text>&gt;</xsl:text>
</xsl:if>
</fo:block>
<fo:block font-size=“11pt” font-family=“serif” start-indent=“0.5in” end-indent=“0.5in”>
<xsl:value-of select=“annotation”/>
</fo:block>
</fo:block>
</xsl:template>
</xsl:stylesheet>
```

This stylesheet produces a PDF document that looks like figure 22.

Actually, it's not quite that simple for PDF documents, because in this case you have to make use of XSLFO. If we look at the “guide2fo.xsl” stylesheet, we see that mostly it looks like the ones we have seen so far, with the important exception that it has an additional namespace declared: fo. The fo namespace marks those elements that are used in XSLFO to determine layout on a printed page. What we actually produce from the transformation is a document marked up with fo formatting tags; we then need some software to render the fo document as a PDF. In this case, I used FOP from the Apache XML project. This apparently two-step transformation (XML to FO to PDF) is actually no

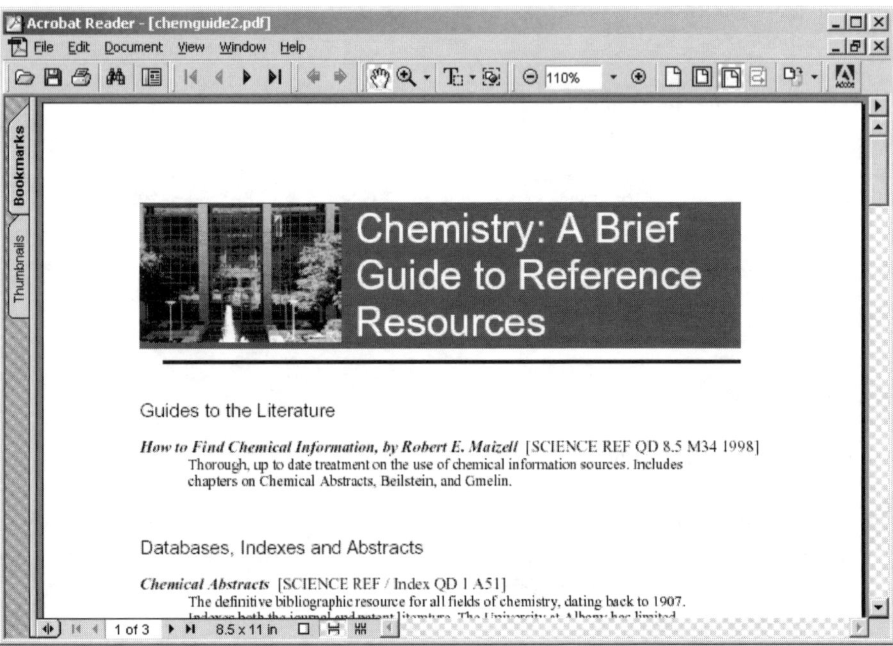

figure 22: Result of transforming a subject guide XML document into a PDF file using another XSL stylesheet.

more complex than what we have been doing with XML to HTML transformations. The difference is that in the latter case, the browser effectively hides the second, rendering phase.

The XML files used for this project were marked up in a simple *ad hoc* XML flavor that I made up for the occasion, but I'd like to say a quick word here about DocBook, which is an XML language originally designed for software documentation, but which is really suitable for almost any type of prose information (but not appropriate for the kind of textual analysis that TEI allows). Having worked a little bit with DocBook, I think it could be of great use in libraries for writing instructional materials, and since it is XML it could also easily be transformed for Web presentation or used for printed manuals. See www.docbook.org for DocBook documentation.

chapter #

XML and Databases

Throughout this book, you have probably found yourself thinking that a lot of this material sounds more like database talk than like Web talk. Indeed, a lot of the examples we have looked at (menus, street addresses, lists of books) seem more like "data" than like "documents." A number of years ago, a developer named Ronald Bourret started discussing XML documents as being data-centric or document-centric and the terminology has stuck. I think most of us have an intuitive sense of what he means by this: there's a big difference between using XML to express your list of customers or employees versus using it to mark up Homeric epics. Typically, for instructional purposes, I tend to use data-centric examples because they are easier to work with, mostly because they are less likely to contain mixed content (child elements interspersed with text).

One of the remarkable things about XML is that it *can* accommodate either documents or data. (As compared, for instance, to a typical desktop computing environment where a document is either a word-processing file OR a spreadsheet, rarely a hybrid.) This is especially nice for applications like EAD, since one could probably start a big fight among archivists by asking them whether a finding aid is a text or a data set. One application that I have worked with a bit is marking up botanical works in XML, which is another case of a hybrid: looked at one way, a flora is an orderly hierarchical listing of plants with fairly terse and predictable descriptive data; looked at another way it is a work of prose with typographical conventions, pagination, prefaces, footnotes, etc.

Let's begin by looking at an example of how a data-centric XML document can be used on the Web in a database-like way (see figure 23). This is the result of some work I did at the University at Albany with Marjorie Benedict, who has compiled a considerable bibliography of critical works about the Canadian novelist Gabrielle Roy. Marjorie marked up the bibliography in XML and I set about building interfaces that would allow it to be searched and displayed in various ways.

From this screen, users have the option of viewing the entire source document displayed in HTML (created on the server via an XSLT transformation) (see figure 24), or

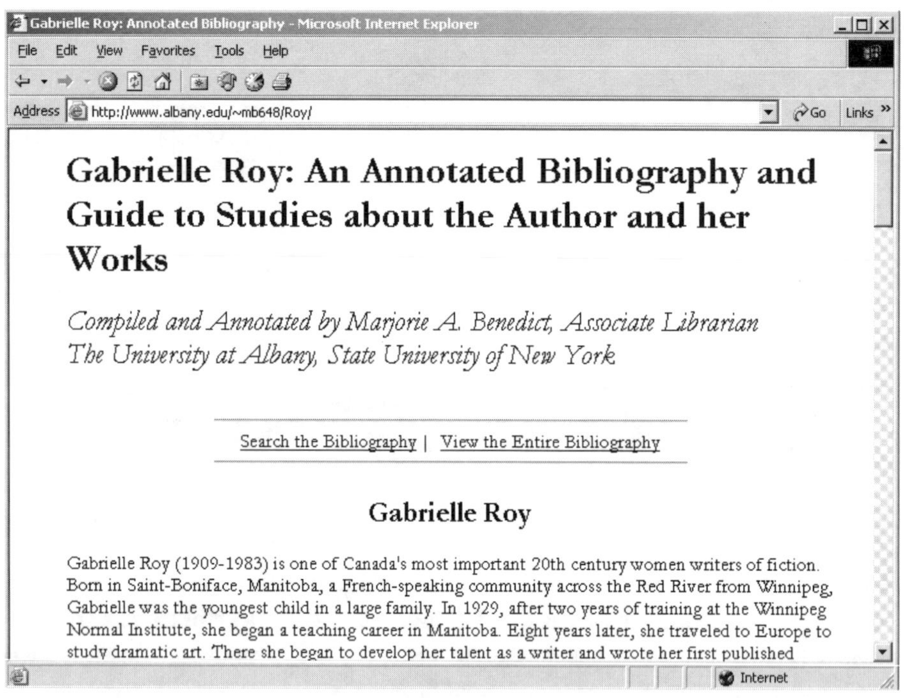

figure 23: Gabrielle Roy bibliography start page.

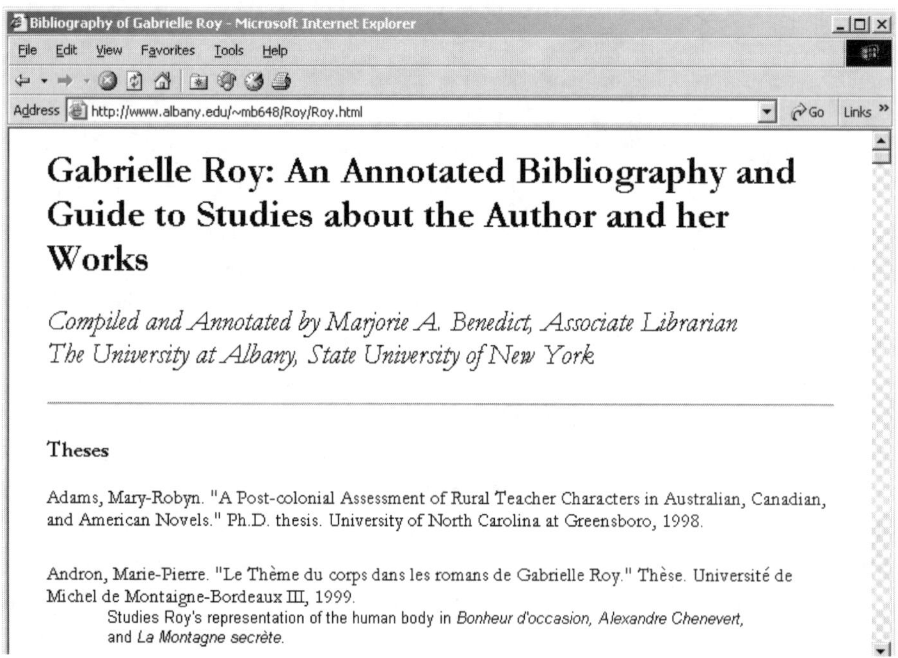

figure 24: HTML version of the Roy bibliography generated using an XSL stylesheet.

of doing a field-specific search (see figure 25). The search is performed by a cgi script, although I also wrote a Java applet as an alternate (faster) approach.

So much for proof of concept: you can make an XML document work more or less like a database back-end on a Web page. There are a few problems with this approach, most importantly speed. Even with a really fast connection, a search in this database takes a few seconds. This brings us to what I would consider the number one thing that databases can do that XML can't: indexing. No matter what kind of brilliant search algorithm I write, the XML parser still has to read through the whole XML file one byte at a time from beginning to end. A binary database management system (like mySQL), wouldn't have to do this—it could look at the search string and sort of "jump" to the appropriate part of the file.

A second thing that a database management system (DBMS) can do that XML can't is data-typing. I've alluded already to the correlation between efficiency and predictability in markup languages. In the case of databases, this rule applies to storage. If the DBMS "knows" that the ISSN field will never contain anything other than exactly 8 digits, it "knows" that it doesn't need to reserve any spare space for data from that field. In "normal" XML (by which I mean XML used with a DTD), you have very limited data typing. For instance, if I code an element as containing PCDATA, there's no way for the parser to know in advance if it will contain a person's surname or the entirety of *Beowulf.* Even for attributes, where the situation is slightly better, we may be able to say that the value will be "yes," "no," or "maybe," but we can't say that the value will be a letter followed by two digits.

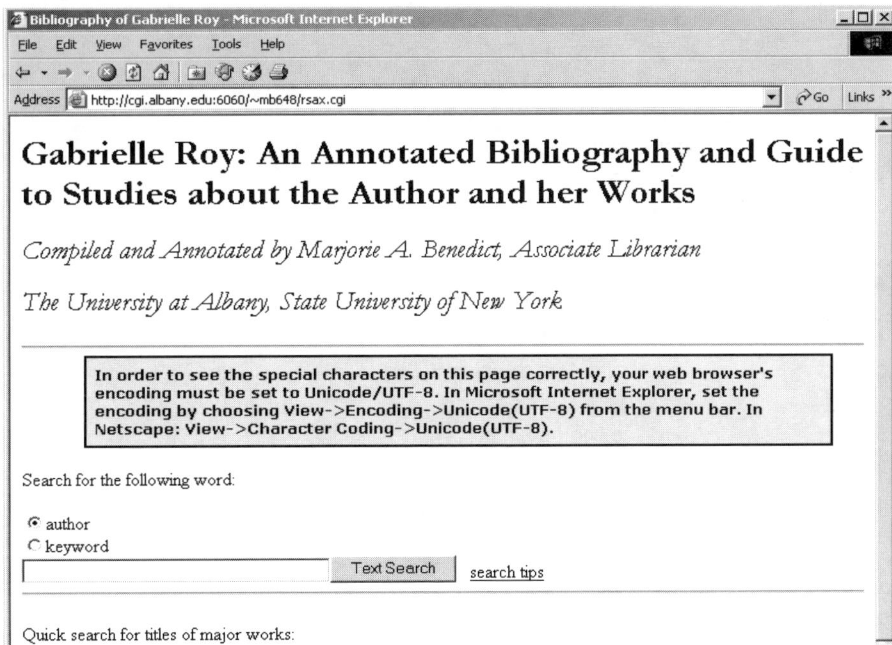

figure 25: Query screen for the Roy bibliography: an example of a searchable XML file.

Remember that back when we first discussed validity, I mentioned the idea of a schema, and said that DTDs are the most common way of expressing schema type information for use with XML. But there are other ways, and this is a very exciting area of activity right now. These new technologies generally make use of XML itself as the format. That way a validating parser only has to be able to read XML, not both XML and DTD. Most of these efforts call themselves schemas, which is confusing because some folks use schema to refer to any representation of structural data for an XML document, while others reserve the term for non-DTD representations. Almost all of these allow some degree of data typing, sometimes quite sophisticated.

As a very simple example, here is an XML encoded discography of the British band King Crimson:

```
<?xml version="1.0" encoding="UTF-8"?>
<discography for="King Crimson"
 xmlns:xsi='www.w3.org/2001/XMLSchema-instance'
 xsi:noNamespaceSchemaLocation='discography3.xsd'>
<album title="In the Court of the Crimson King" year="1969">
		<song>21st Century Schizoid Man</song>
		<song>I Talk to the Wind</song>
		<song>Epitaph</song>
		<song>Moonchild</song>
		<song>Court of the Crimson King</song>
	</album>
	<album title="In the Wake of Poseidon" year="1970">
		<song>Peace: A Beginning</song>
		<song>Pictures of a City</song>
		<song>Cadence and Cascade</song>
		<song>In the Wake of Poseidon</song>
		<song>Peace: A Theme</song>
		<song>Catfood</song>
		<song>The Devil&apos;s Triangle</song>
		<song>Peace: An End</song>
	</album>
	<album title="Lizard" year="1970">
		<song>Cirkus</song>
		<song>Indoor Games</song>
		<song>Happy Family</song>
		<song>Lady of the Dancing Waters</song>
		<song>Lizard</song>
	</album>
	<album title="Islands" year="1971">
		<song>Formentera Lady</song>
		<song>Sailor&apos;s Tale</song>
		<song>The Letter</song>
		<song>Ladies of the Road</song>
		<song>Song of the Gulls</song>
		<song>Islands</song>
	</album>
```

```
        <album title="Larks Tongues in Aspic" year="1973">
                <song>Larks Tongues in Aspic Part I</song>
                <song>Book of Saturday</song>
                <song>Exiles</song>
                <song>Easy Money</song>
                <song>The Talking Drum</song>
                <song>Larks Tongues in Aspic Part II</song>
        </album>
        <album title="Starless and Bible Black" year="1974">
                <song>Great Deciever</song>
                <song>Lament</song>
                <song>We&apos;ll let you know</song>
                <song>Trio</song>
                <song>The Night Watch</song>
                <song>Starless and Bible Black</song>
                <song>Fracture</song>
        </album>
        <album title="Red" year="1975">
                <song>Red</song>
                <song>Fallen Angel</song>
                <song>One More Red Nightmare</song>
                <song>Providence</song>
                <song>Starless</song>
        </album>
</discography>
```

Here is a very simple XML Schema (when you see "XML Schema" with a capital "S," that refers to the W3C's schema standard) for a discography:

```
<?xml version="1.0" encoding="UTF-8"?>
<xs:schema xmlns:xs="www.w3.org/2001/XMLSchema">
<!—This schema uses the data type design. —>
<!—Define simple type elements so that you can use them later —>
<xs:simpleType name="nameType">
 <xs:restriction base="xs:string"/>
</xs:simpleType>
<xs:simpleType name="forType">
 <xs:restriction base="xs:string">
 <xs:maxLength value="32"/>
 </xs:restriction>
</xs:simpleType>
<xs:simpleType name="yearType">
 <xs:restriction base="xs:gYear"/>
</xs:simpleType>
<!—Define complex type elements with reference to the simple types —>
<xs:complexType name="albumType">
 <xs:sequence>
 <xs:element name="song" type="nameType" maxOccurs="unbounded"/>
 </xs:sequence>
 <xs:attribute name="title" type="nameType" use="required"/>
```

```
  <xs:attribute name="year" type="yearType" use="required"/>
 </xs:complexType>
 <xs:complexType name="discographyType">
  <xs:sequence>
  <xs:element name="album" type="albumType" maxOccurs="unbounded"/>
  </xs:sequence>
  <xs:attribute name="for" type="forType" use="required"/>
 </xs:complexType>
 <!—Reference to discographyType to define the discography element —>
 <xs:element name="discography" type="discographyType"/>
 </xs:schema>
```

Notice that there is an element:

```
<xs:simpleType name="yearType">
 <xs:restriction base="xs:gYear" />
</xs:simpleType>
```

This states that elements or attributes which are designated as being of "yearType" must use the format defined as xs:gYear (Gregorian year) in the XML Schema spec. Then later in the document the attribute with the name "year" is defined as having a type attribute of "yearType," and so falls under that rule:

```
<xs:attribute name="year" type="yearType" use="required"/>
```

IE will not validate against XML Schemas, so some other parser is needed to check validity. In figure 26 the King Crimson file displayed in the commercial editor XMLSPY.

The green check mark indicates that the document is valid. If I change the value of year for the *Wake of Poseidon* album to "ohio" and run the validator again, I see figure 27.

The red "X" indicates a validity problem, with the message "This file is not valid: Invalid value for datatype gYear in attribute 'year.'" This datatyping capability also allows the use of regular expressions, which are strings of symbols used to match lines of text. Here is an example of a regular expression from the MARCXML schema, designating a pattern which consists of two zeros followed by either a single digit or a single letter of either case:

```
<xsd:pattern value="00[1-9A-Za-z]{1}"/>
```

So, XML's apparent lack of datatyping is really a failure of DTDs and is being remedied by newer standards.

Efficiency of storage can be another area where XML falls short relative to DBMS technology. Storing tons of data as flat text, as it is in XML, is not very efficient compared to the data storage techniques of DBMSs. Of course, we all know that disc space is cheap, so for many purposes (especially for less-than-enormous projects), this really isn't much of a consideration.

Finally, most DBMSs provide a lot of very important features covering issues like security, multiple accesses, and data integrity checks that you're not going to get by using do-it-yourself XML. (Of course, we have seen and will see a lot of XML-backed database tools that may offer some of these features.)

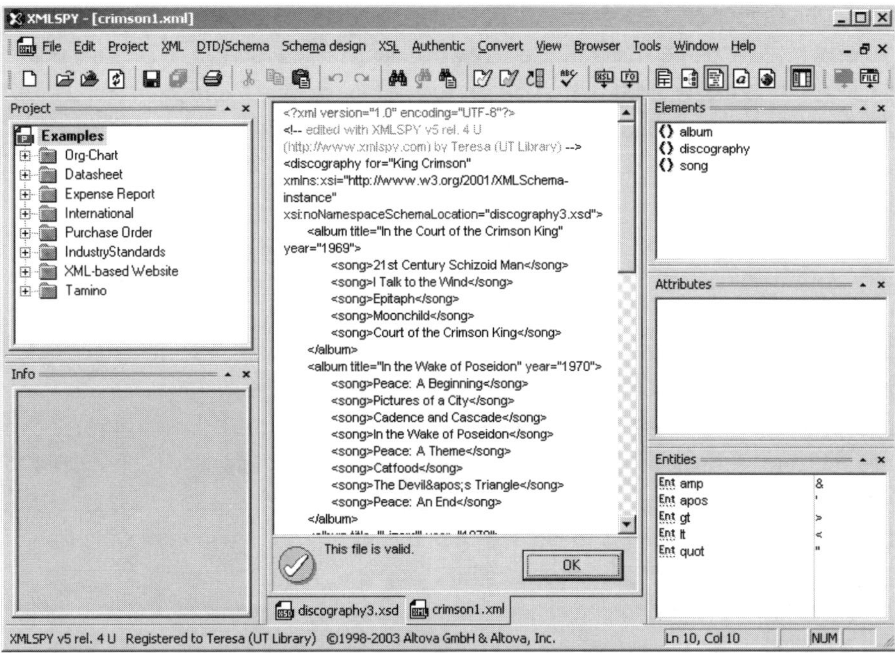

figure 26: King Crimson document validating successfully against its XML Schema in XMLSPY.

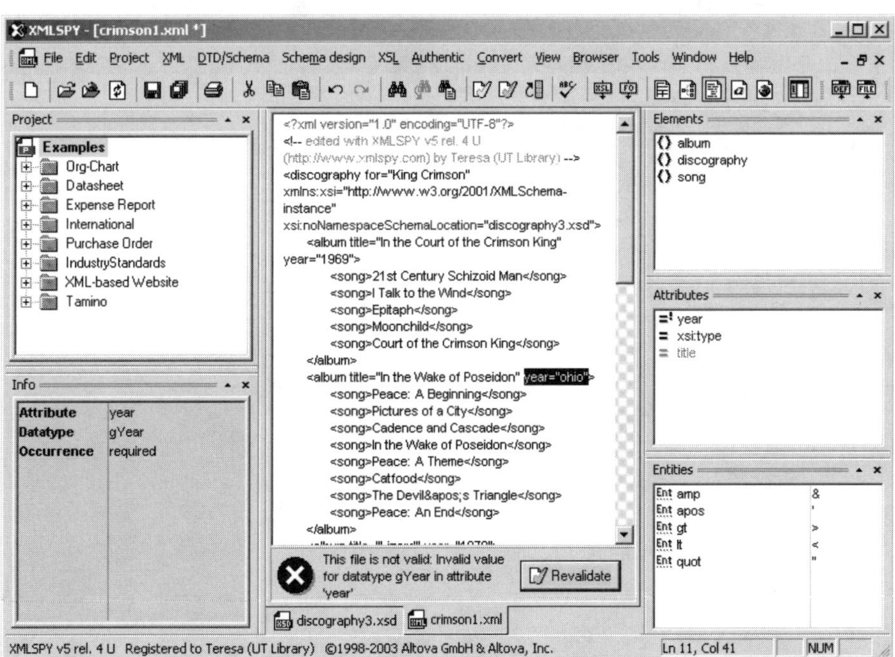

figure 27: King Crimson document failing Schema validation in XMLSPY.

So, having extolled the virtues of XML for some pages, I am now telling you all the things that XML can't do that MS Access and similar familiar tools can. What's my point?

My point is that while XML has a major role in the realm of information technology, it is not going to replace the DBMS. Its major role will be the transport of data rather than storage. When looked at in juxtaposition to a fully-fledged DBMS, XML may look like a poor relation, but it has one huge advantage: portability. It can be used on any computing platform, with any major programming language, and increasingly can be used as a transfer format between DBMSs. This in itself has some advantages.

Let's take a hypothetical case in which we have six different database formats that are used in our library (not as far-fetched as you might think). If these systems needed to share information, our programmers would need to write 6^2-6 = 30 filters to interconvert between the systems (see figure 28). On the other hand, if we make use of a neutral "hub" format for information transfer, our programmers would only need to write 2 x 6 = 12 filters (see figure 29). XML is ideal for use in this role because of it combines cross-platform utility with the degree of complexity needed to model the kind of data often stored in relational databases.

There has been quite a bit written about how to code relational data in XML, and I am not going to go too deeply into this. I will show you a quick example of how this is often done:

```
<?xml version="1.0"?>
<!DOCTYPE quartets [
        <!ELEMENT quartets (composers_table, works_table)>
        <!ELEMENT composers_table (composer+)>
        <!ELEMENT composer (fname, lname, bdate, ddate)>
        <!ATTLIST composer id ID #REQUIRED>
        <!ELEMENT fname (#PCDATA)>
        <!ELEMENT lname (#PCDATA)>
        <!ELEMENT bdate (#PCDATA)>
        <!ELEMENT ddate (#PCDATA)>
        <!ELEMENT works_table (work+)>
        <!ELEMENT work (title, composer_ref, opus?, composition_year)>
        <!ATTLIST work id ID #REQUIRED>
        <!ELEMENT title (#PCDATA)>
        <!ELEMENT composer_ref EMPTY>
        <!ATTLIST composer_ref ref IDREF #REQUIRED>
        <!ELEMENT opus (#PCDATA)>
        <!ELEMENT composition_year (#PCDATA)>
]>
<quartets>
<composers_table>
<composer id="c1">
        <fname>Joseph</fname>
        <lname>Haydn</lname>
        <bdate>1732</bdate>
        <ddate>1809</ddate>
```

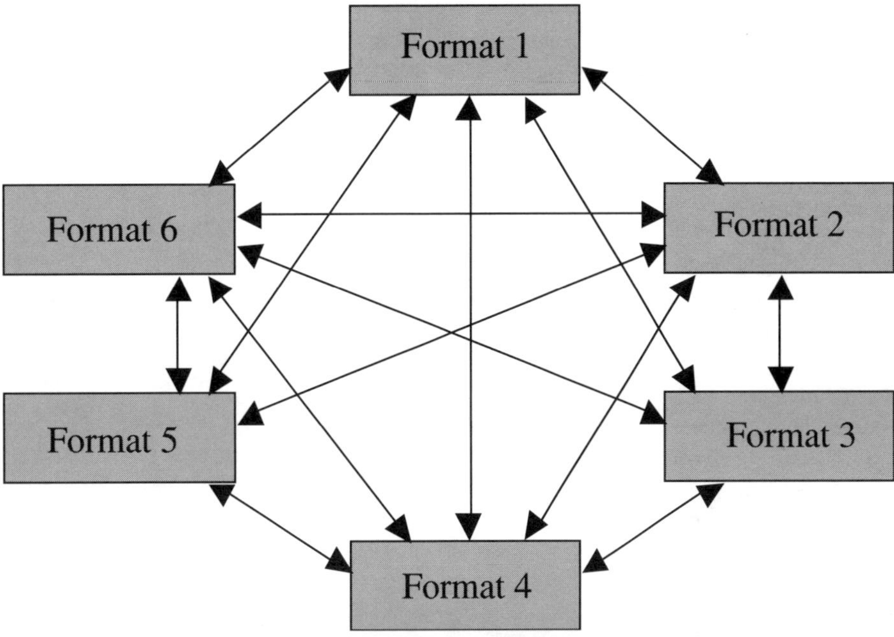

figure 28: No central hub format: for n formats, n2-n filter programs are needed to interconvert (here, 30).

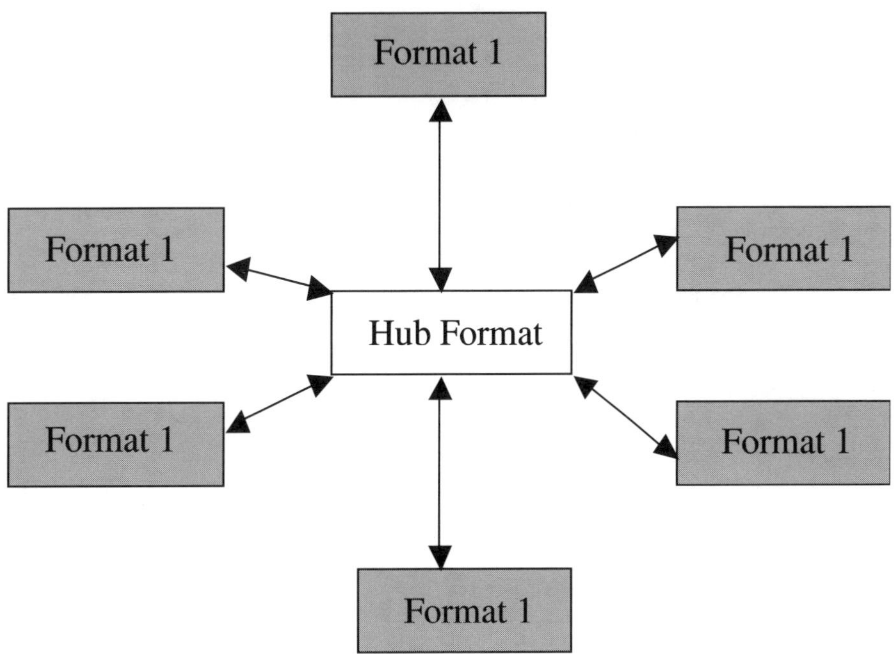

figure 29: With a hub format: for n formats, only 2n filters are needed to interconvert (here, 12).

```
</composer>
<composer id="c2">
        <fname>Ludwig Van</fname>
        <lname>Beethoven</lname>
        <bdate>1770</bdate>
        <ddate>1827</ddate>
</composer>
<composer id="c3">
        <fname>Felix</fname>
        <lname>Mendelssohn</lname>
        <bdate>1809</bdate>
        <ddate>1847</ddate>
</composer>
<composer id="c4">
        <fname>Paul</fname>
        <lname>Hindemith</lname>
        <bdate>1895</bdate>
        <ddate>1963</ddate>
</composer>
<composer id="c5">
        <fname>Bela</fname>
        <lname>Bartok</lname>
        <bdate>1881</bdate>
        <ddate>1945</ddate>
</composer>
<composer id="c6">
        <fname>Leos</fname>
        <lname>Janacek</lname>
        <bdate>1854</bdate>
        <ddate>1928</ddate>
</composer>
<composer id="c7">
        <fname>Benjamin</fname>
        <lname>Britten</lname>
        <bdate>1913</bdate>
        <ddate>1976</ddate>
</composer>
</composers_table>
<works_table>
<work id="w1">
        <title>String Quartet No. 1 'Kreutzer'</title>
        <composer_ref ref="c6"/>
        <composition_year>1923</composition_year>
</work>
<work id="w2">
        <title>String Quartet No. 2 'Lettres intimes'</title>
        <composer_ref ref="c6"/>
        <composition_year>1928</composition_year>
</work>
```

```
<work id="w3">
	<title>String Quartet No. 1</title>
	<composer_ref ref="c5"/>
	<opus>7</opus>
	<composition_year>1909</composition_year>
</work>
<work id="w4">
	<title>String Quartet No. 2</title>
	<composer_ref ref="c5"/>
	<opus>17</opus>
	<composition_year>1917</composition_year>
</work>
<work id="w5">
	<title>String Quartet No. 3</title>
	<composer_ref ref="c5"/>
	<composition_year>1927</composition_year>
</work>
<work id="w6">
	<title>String Quartet No. 4</title>
	<composer_ref ref="c5"/>
	<composition_year>1928</composition_year>
</work>
<work id="w7">
	<title>String Quartet No. 5</title>
	<composer_ref ref="c5"/>
	<composition_year>1934</composition_year>
</work>
<work id="w8">
	<title>String Quartet No. 6</title>
	<composer_ref ref="c5"/>
	<composition_year>1939</composition_year>
</work>
<work id="w9">
	<title>String Quartet No. 0</title>
	<composer_ref ref="c4"/>
	<opus>2</opus>
	<composition_year>1915</composition_year>
</work>
<work id="w10">
	<title>String Quartet No. 3</title>
	<composer_ref ref="c4"/>
	<opus>22</opus>
	<composition_year>1922</composition_year>
</work>
<work id="w11">
	<title>String Quartet No. 4</title>
	<composer_ref ref="c4"/>
	<opus>32</opus>
	<composition_year>1923</composition_year>
```

```
</work>
<work id="w12">
        <title>String Quartet No. 5 in E-flat</title>
        <composer_ref ref="c4"/>
        <composition_year>1943</composition_year>
</work>
<work id="w13">
        <title>Militarminimax</title>
        <composer_ref ref="c4"/>
        <composition_year>1923</composition_year>
</work>
<work id="w14">
        <title>String Quartet in E-flat</title>
        <composer_ref ref="c3"/>
        <opus>12</opus>
        <composition_year>1829</composition_year>
</work>
<work id="w15">
        <title>String Quartet in a</title>
        <composer_ref ref="c3"/>
        <opus>13</opus>
        <composition_year>1827</composition_year>
</work>
<work id="w16">
        <title>String Quartet in F</title>
        <composer_ref ref="c2"/>
        <opus>18.1</opus>
        <composition_year>1799</composition_year>
</work>
<work id="w17">
        <title>String Quartet in E-flat</title>
        <composer_ref ref="c2"/>
        <opus>127</opus>
        <composition_year>1824</composition_year>
</work>
<work id="w18">
        <title>String Quartet in G</title>
        <composer_ref ref="c2"/>
        <opus>18.2</opus>
        <composition_year>1799</composition_year>
</work>
<work id="w19">
        <title>String Quartet in B-flat</title>
        <composer_ref ref="c2"/>
        <opus>130</opus>
        <composition_year>1826</composition_year>
</work>
<work id="w20">
        <title>String Quartet in b</title>
```

```
        <composer_ref ref="c1"/>
        <opus>33.1</opus>
        <composition_year>1781</composition_year>
</work>
<work id="w21">
        <title>String Quartet in E-flat 'The Joke'</title>
        <composer_ref ref="c1"/>
        <opus>33.2</opus>
        <composition_year>1781</composition_year>
</work>
<work id="w22">
        <title>String Quartet in B-flat</title>
        <composer_ref ref="c1"/>
        <opus>33.4</opus>
        <composition_year>1781</composition_year>
</work>
<work id="w23">
        <title>String Quartet in C 'The Bird'</title>
        <composer_ref ref="c1"/>
        <opus>33.3</opus>
        <composition_year>1781</composition_year>
</work>
<work id="w24">
        <title>String Quartet in G</title>
        <composer_ref ref="c1"/>
        <opus>33.5</opus>
        <composition_year>1781</composition_year>
</work>
<work id="w25">
        <title>String Quartet in D</title>
        <composer_ref ref="c1"/>
        <opus>33.6</opus>
        <composition_year>1781</composition_year>
</work>
</works_table>
</quartets>
```

In database terms, this document contains two "tables," one for composers and one for string quartets. Composers are uniquely identified by an ID-type attribute (creatively named "id"). The "work" element has a "composer_ref" attribute of type IDREF. The composers can then be referred to from within a "work" element through the "ref" attribute of the "composer_ref" attribute.

This is a very simple example, but it is possible to model fairly elaborate relational data in XML, which of course makes it possible for DBMSs to read and write XML data, allowing it to serve the "hub" function for which it is so well suited.

We can look at the XML versus DBMS scenario as a special case of how XML relates to other information formats in general. I've generalized this concept into a highly unscientific concept of "thermodynamics of information" (see figure 30).

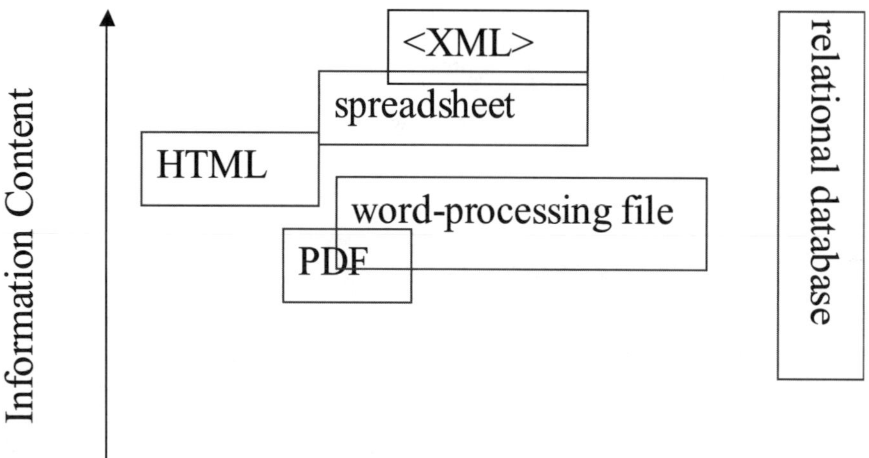

figure 30: Relative information content of various file types.

At least once as you've read this book, you have probably found yourself thinking "yes, I could do it that way, but is this really better than the way I've been doing it?" (This type of thinking likely showed up when I told you how much better XML is than HTML and then went on to tell you about an exciting technology called XSL that will turn your XML back into HTML again.) I'd like now to present a sort of IT cosmology that I think may help you think about the long term usefulness of various file types. This graphic shows a number of common file types that we all work with arranged with a vague concept called "information content" increasing toward the top of the graph. If we have data that we would like to move between various formats, it is easy to go "downhill" and hard to go "uphill." You can probably come up with an automated process of some sort to dump your XML data into a PDF document, but you'd have a hard time writing a program to get data from a PDF document into a spreadsheet. Going all the way back to Chapter 1, this is at least in part because of the purely descriptive nature of PDF markup. If you are an archivist with your finding aids in EAD, it's fairly trivial to convert them to HTML, but if you have them in HTML, you'll likely be looking at some serious hand-coding to get them into EAD.

So, if I can leave you with one big point about the value of XML, it is that once you have your information in XML, you likely have all that you need, since you can always go "downhill" to derivative formats. You'll notice that the thorn in the side of my XML-rules-the-world cosmology is relational database technology. This is because a good DBMS can be as smart or smarter than XML, which is one reason that "XML and Databases" rated a whole chapter. I can confidently tell you that keeping data in XML rather than HTML or Word documents is a good idea, but in talking about XML versus a good DBMS, you really need to weigh the pros and cons for your individual needs.

What You Can Do at Home

One of the great things about XML as a technology is that you can experiment with it a great deal without much in the way of software. These are some things you may want to have on your computer to make your XML experiments easier (listed from most to least essential):

Microsoft Internet Explorer 6—I specifically recommend version 6 or later because of its support for XSL. Previous versions of IE (5.x) supported an earlier version of XSL. The XSL examples in this book *will not work* with IE 5.x.

Internet Explorer Tools for Validating XML and Viewing XSLT Output—This is a small bundle of files that will allow you to use Internet Explorer to check the validity of XML files against DTDs and will also allow you to see the output of your XSL transformations. These are very useful tools for beginners. Download the tools from ww.microsoft.com/downloads/details.aspx?FamilyId=D23C1D2C-1571-4D61-BDA8-ADF9F6849DF9&displaylang=en. *Follow the directions carefully*—this is an unusual download.

A Good Text Editor—I use NoteTab Light, which is available for free at www.notetab.com. This is a simple text editor that you can use for writing XML, DTDs, stylesheets, HTML, etc. It has a "view in browser" button so that you can quickly see the results of your labors in a browser (make sure your default browser is IE6!). It also offers customizable "clipbooks" of tags so that you can have "point and click" access to elements that you create.

XML tools from Apache (Xerces, Xalan, FOP)—These are recommended for those who are serious about XML and who are comfortable dealing with Java software and have the Java 2 development kit installed. All of these tools are available for free download (as binary or source code) from the Apache XML Project (http://xml.apache.org). Java is available from Sun Microsystems at http://java.sun.com.

An XML editor—If you feel compelled to spend money, XMLSPY is an excellent choice and will allow you to do some things that would otherwise be difficult to manage on your desktop computer, such as XSLFO transformations and validation against XML Schemas. This is available for a free 30-day evaluation period from Altova (www.altova.com). The cost is $399.

XML Resources

On The Web

General XML Sites

W3C (www.w3.org)

This W3C (World Wide Web Consortium) is the organization that developed XML and is the closest thing there is to a body that is "in charge of" the Web. All of the formal specifications are available on this site, as well as some tutorials and guidelines.

xml.com (www.xml.com)

This site is produced by O'Reilly (the publisher that brings us all those great computer books with the animal woodcuts on the covers) and is a great site for keeping up with XML news and the ever-expanding constellation of technologies that surround XML.

Cover Pages (www.oasis-open.org/cover/sgml-xml.html)

A wonderfully comprehensive (to the point of overwhelming) site on all things related to XML. One of the very best places to investigate specific XML applications.

Specific XML Applications

Encoded Archival Description (www.loc.gov/ead)

This is an example of a very specific XML application, designed for use with archival finding aids.

The Text Encoding Initiative (www.tei-c.org)

Very flexible XML application designed for the scholarly analysis of texts. The DTD is huge, but users may customize the DTD by choosing the exact sections that they need for specific types of texts (e.g., poetry, plays, etc.).

Open Archives Initiative (www.openarchives.org)
A project that encourages the free sharing of XML-encoded metadata (usually Dublin Core) about electronic collections among member institutions.

MARC in XML from the Library of Congress (www.loc.gov/marc/marcxml.html)
LOC's intitiative for an XML encoding of MARC records, with downloadable DTD and XML Schema.

Medlane XMLMARC (http://xmlmarc.stanford.edu)
Another experiment in expressing MARC records in XML syntax.

Dublin Core Metadata Initiative (http://dublincore.org)
Dublin Core is not itself an XML application (since XML is a syntax and DC is syntax-independent), but it is most often used in an XML context.

In Print

Harold, Elliott Rusty. 2001. *The XML Bible*, 2d ed. New York: Hungry Minds.
This is my favorite XML book on the market, largely because it serves well both as an introduction and as a reference work once you know what you're doing.

Ray, Eric T. 2001. *Learning XML*. O'Reilly.
Very good, *concise* (this is a rarity in computer books) guide to get you started with XML.

Means, W. Scott, and Elliott Rusty Harold. 2001. *XML in a Nutshell*. O'Reilly.
This is a reference book (in the format of O'Reilly's other Nutshell manuals), so is not really intended for the complete novice. This is great to have on hand so you can look up those features that you use less frequently.

St. Laurent, Simon. 2000. *XML Elements of Style*. New York: McGraw-Hill.
This is a wonderful *second* XML book. It is not the best introduction, but has a lot to say about how to write *good* XML, once you know how to write XML.

Tennant, Roy, ed. 2002. *XML in Libraries*. New York: Neal-Schuman Publishers.
Compilation of contributed papers on practical uses of XML in libraries, ranging from cataloging to interlibary loan and electronic publication.

Tittel, Ed, Natanya Pitts, and Frank Boumphrey. 2002. *XML for Dummies*, 3d ed. New York: Hungry Minds.
Not the best XML book overall, but contains very good, up-to-date discussions of some current uses of XML (an area in which some of the more "academic" books are weak).

Date Due

JUN 17 2005			
IL 98813945			2.14.13

BRODART, CO. Cat. No. 23-233-003 Printed in U.S.A.